QUAKER PEGG

GEORGE DRURY

PUBLISHED BY THE AUTHOR
2011

First published by George Drury in 2011

A CIP catalogue record for this book
is available from the British Library.

ISBN 978-0-9568910-0-6

CONTENTS

Acknowledgements

I am in debt to Rose and the late Eric Sandford for the loan of books and for guiding me to the Quaker archives. Rose, at 99 still as sharp as ever, maintains her enthusiastic support. The late John Fineran gave me quiet encouragement over many years and provided invaluable advice after reading an early draft of the text. Very shortly before he died, John saw this final version and it is because of his excited response to the Pegg portrait that it figures prominently on the cover. Anne Dunne at the Derby Museum and Art Gallery could not have been more helpful, particularly over facilitating the photography of pieces from their collection. The Hon. Hugh Gibson was equally kind and generous in supplying photographs of pages from the Sketch Book now in the Crown Derby Museum. Mrs. Joan Shaw showed immediate interest and encouragement, allowing photographs of the Pegg portrait, which she owns. The staff at Derby Local Studies Library have been most helpful and Nick Tomlinson of Derbyshire Library Service made it easy to use photographs from Picturethepast, that wonderful user-friendly archive for Nottinghamshire and Derbyshire. I am grateful to the private collector for permitting photographs on pages 37 and 51. My son Paul and my daughter Isabel have given me tremendous support. Isabel took some of the remaining unacknowleged photographs. Finally, my gratitude to my patient wife Erica who checked the grammar, made no comment on the text but simply laughs whenever the words 'Quaker Pegg' come up in our conversations.

Introduction

When you first arrive to live somewhere and you start to look around, you visit places in the first few weeks you may hardly ever visit again. When I first came to Derbyshire fifty years ago, I looked in at the local museum in Derby. My memory of the generally unexciting impression it made is no doubt unkind but it seemed to consist of a strange mixture of stuffed birds, grey bits of broken pottery, a few faded military uniforms and a large case containing a model railway. And then there was the collection of Derby Porcelain and Royal Crown Derby. This was crammed together and I didn't like it much: the earlier stuff fussy, the later all gold, claret and dark navy blue, the worst type of Victorian excess. However, in the middle of this accumulation I came across a square white plate. Exploding on it, barely confined within the plate, was a thistle. I remember feeling as if I had taken a short cut across wasteland and had suddenly been scratched by a real thistle. The curling card at the side said something like this.

'Thistle Plate: William 'Quaker' Pegg 1775 to 1851. As a young man Pegg collected the original thistle on Nuns Green in Derby one Whitsun Holiday and drew it. He was encouraged to paint the design on this dish and it was kept for many years at the factory. Pegg was troubled constantly by his religious scruples and gave up painting shortly afterwards when he became a Quaker in 1800. He returned to work again at the Derby Factory from 1813 to 1820.'

After a lapse of some time I visited the gallery again. By now the plate was displayed, not in a shadowy case but in a new gallery with space around it and properly lit. Indeed, the stuff I had hastily dismissed so long before, looked better too. Just a little further along was a plain white plate with a gorgeous blue gentian flower above surging leaves and it even had roots wriggling around underneath. It was obviously by the same artist with the same intensity and the same dramatic presentation. I was reminded of the bare details in the explanatory note. What was intriguing was the contradiction between the exuberance of the decoration and the severe rejection of any form of painting at all. It seemed to me that the intensity and the style of his work could well be the direct result of such conflicting pressures and had created something rather special. This was my incentive to examine these pressures in detail and, indeed at last, to find out more about his life and work.

1: John Haslem and Quaker Pegg

The place to begin, if you are familiar with Derby, is the middle of St. Mary's Bridge, facing downstream. Looking to your left, between you and the modern bridge that carries the dual carriageway, you see a grass slope. Now, imagine the slope has evaporated and instead you see the entrance to a canal, branching off from the main river, to the right of Nottingham Road. Next you have to imagine that you are standing on the bridge on the afternoon of the first of January 1850. A man walks briskly towards and past you. You glimpse a pleasant face, neatly trimmed moustache, side- whiskers, an elegant tailcoat, top hat. He hurries, possibly because of the cold, but mainly because he is excited. In his hand he carries a small brown paper parcel. He goes down the gravelly slope beside the canal and into Nottingham Road, casting a meaningful glance at the newly built, red brick building which juts out a hundred yards or so in front of him, before he turns abruptly across the street shortly before the point where a small footbridge crosses the canal and goes into a tiny shop, packed in amongst the houses.

We would call this 'a corner-shop'; the man would have called it 'a huckster's store'. Inside let us imagine flour sacks, with tops rolled back, vegetables in wickerwork baskets, pans hanging on the walls and facing us a wooden counter. Behind it waits a slightly stooping, white-haired elderly man in a grey apron. You notice one eye half closed. Behind him there are shelves with rows of jars with neat, hand-written labels. To his right is a hock of ham on a white plate with a broad blade knife at its side. The elegant gentleman has the parcel in his hand. "Mr. William Pegg?" he enquires. "I am, sir". "I wonder whether you recognise this?" He takes the paper off his parcel to reveal our Thistle Dish.

From now on we have no need to imagine what happened, since the elegant gentleman, John Haslem, has described it for us.

'As soon as he saw it, he began in his quiet manner to relate how that more than fifty years before he had gathered the original of that thistle, a Lady Thistle, it was called, while making a walk in Nun's Green one Whitsun holidays (sic) – how he first made a pencil sketch of it, - how that on his mother, when she saw the sketch, saying she could make nothing of it, he said "I'll show thee, then", and he coloured it, and when he shewed the drawing to Thomas Soar, the overlooker of the painters, he gave him that dish to paint it on.'

Haslem explains that the dish was subsequently kept at the China Works 'as a study for the flower painters and was highly prized by them' for the next 48 years until the factory closed. He had managed to track it down that morning and had bought it for four shillings. 'The dish is slightly cracked, and if it ever had any gilding on it, it is all worn off, but the thistle is as fresh and pure as when first painted'.

Although Haslem had lived in London for the previous 15 years, this small patch of Derby, Nottingham Road, the footbridge over the canal, the two courts (short rows of terraced houses running at right angles to the main road) next to the shop,[*1] was as familiar for him as anywhere else in the world. This explains that 'meaningful' and probably sad, glance towards the freshly built, red brick gable end of the substantial structure further up the road, the Convent of St. Vincent of Paul. Five years before, on that site stood an even larger collection of buildings, encircling a number of pot-bellied kilns. This was the Derby Porcelain Factory. As a child, Haslem had come to live with his uncle, James Thomason, who was the general manager of the works. He writes: "The little shop was well known to (me) in those by-gone days, and much of (my) small coin did (I) invest in buns and butter-scotch, in the making of which tempting articles Mrs. Pegg had no equal according to (my) juvenile judgment".

At the age of 14 in 1822 Haslem became an apprentice china painter. He remained there for the next 13 years until he moved to a studio in London where he adapted his skills to painting enamels. The studio had royal patronage and before long he was meeting commissions from Queen Victoria and Prince Albert. However, at the time of his excited visit to Pegg, he was at the very height of his success. The following year, in a competition as part of the Great 1851 Exhibition, his work was rejected by the judges. This was clearly a great disappointment for him, especially as he felt it was the outcome of dubious politicking behind the scenes. He received no more royal commissions. When his aunt died in 1857, his uncle sent plaintive letters asking him to return to Derby and Haslem, a bachelor, had no reason to refuse.

The main project for the rest of his life – he lived another 27 years – was to gather information about the Derby China Factory, interview anyone who worked there and, as we have seen, collect china. You gain the impression from his book 'The Old Derby China Factory' which was published in 1876, that he had a balanced view of his own achievements. He was a provincial at heart and the London experience was only an interlude, albeit a rather fabulous one. He used to tell the story of the day he spent the morning at an audience with the Queen and on his way home on the train encountered 'a poor woman' in a confused panic because she was in the wrong class compartment. He gently guided her to a railway official who sorted her out. "I therefore rendered a trifling service to one of the humblest and held converse with the highest in the realm on the same day."

To go back to our imagined reconstruction of his encounter with Pegg, for him to need to enquire and use the formal address "Mr. William Pegg?" was wrong. Haslem knew him well. After all, his uncle's house (his own past home in Derby) was next door but one to the Peggs', and, despite his fashionable success in London, he had been just as much an everyday pot decorator as Pegg. Reading his book, it is quite clear that his great enthusiasm for the project is really based on his affection for the workforce and the companionship it gave him. The book grew out of a series of reminiscences he had written for the local newspaper. Nothing demonstrates this more clearly than the following passage: first, because no academic history would find any relevance for it and secondly because he has a perfect ear for Derby dialect and accent.

'The warehouse was built shortly after 1811, on the site of what had been a wood-yard. On the sign in front was painted in large letters, "Porcelain Manufactory". One day a painter was engaged in re-lettering this sign. Mr. Bloor and two or three others standing on the other side of the road, looking on, when an odd character, "Georgie" Saxton by name, passed. Mr. Bloor said something to George in a joking way, which that individual did not take in good part, and, turning to Bloor, asked him who he was, adding, "Ah dar sey yo thinken yoresen a big un nah, bur yo wor nowt bur a clark once!" and with an oath, George continued, "Clark-seed grows fast! And a pratty soat of a clark yo mun a bin for yo dunner no hah ter spell pots yet! Look theer" – pointing to the man at work at the sign, and who had just completed the first three letters in Porcelain, "P-O-R is ner t'wey to spell pots" and George went on his way muttering "P-O-R pots".

The full title of Haslem's book was 'The Old Derby China Factory: The Workmen and Their Productions. Containing biographical sketches of the chief artist workmen, the various marks used, fac-similies copied from the old Derby pattern books, the original price list of more than 400 figures and groups, etc. etc.' Out of all the 'chief artist workmen', he devoted more pages to Pegg than to any other. There is a reason for this (which we will give later) and not necessarily because he regarded Pegg as the best or most important. Indeed, he wrote 'Probably the ablest man who may be said to have been produced by the old Derby china works was William Billingsley' whereas William Pegg was 'one of the best flower painters employed at Derby'.

FOOTNOTE

1. Amazingly, in amongst all the subsequent 19th and 20th century building activity in this area, one of these courts still survives and, to my eye, looks much as it would have in Pegg's time (see page 36). The numbers of the houses seem to have fluctuated during the century. During the Peggs' residence theirs was number 3 and Thomason's number 5. Haslem gives the number 40 but this was never the case.

2: Haslem's Account of Pegg's Life

Haslem's account took up 26 full pages but it can be summarised.

Pegg was born near Newcastle-under-Lyme in 1775, the son of a gardener who had worked for some years at Etwall Hall. Father was a Calvinist and made sure that young William attended religious meetings throughout his childhood. At the age of 10 he started work, shovelling fuel into the stoves at an earthenware factory, and five years later became an apprentice painter at a china works. He did his best to study in his spare time but, since he was working 15 hours a day, he can hardly have had much leisure. In 1796, when he was 21, he moved to Derby on a 5 year contract with William Duesbury who owned the Derby China Works. He spent his five years producing many fine works, including the Thistle Plate, but increasingly questioned whether it was morally right to indulge in the luxury of painting natural objects simply for pleasure. Haslem writes 'he was the subject of strange religious scruples'. It was a period of complete appraisal of his religious convictions. He moved from the Calvinists to the Baptists to attending meetings of the Society of Friends (the Quakers) and eventually formally joined them in 1800. This strengthened his misgivings and in 1801 he not only gave up his employment but also burned most of his drawings and paintings.

Pegg now determined to earn his living as a stocking-maker but even here he made sure that this did not include the decorative trimmings which would often be added to the top of the stocking. He lived with his mother in Derby but she found his religious explanations for giving up a secure and lucrative living hard to understand and apparently told him so frequently. He suddenly left to live in Hinckley in Leicestershire, 'considered the rudest and most uncultivated place in many miles', as he explained later. For the next seven years he stayed there and at Bedworth, near Nuneaton, barely earning a living by stocking-making which he tried to supplement by school-teaching, but both ultimately failed. It was a miserable existence, physically and mentally, only sustained by his Quaker Friends but even those in Hinckley and

Bedworth were rather grudging. He moved to Coventry where, if anything, he became even more depressed. At last, he reconsidered his attitude to painting. Haslem's extensive quotations from letters written throughout these years show that Pegg had consistently maintained his connections with Derby.

Pegg suddenly re-appeared at the Derby China Works in 1813. Aged 39, he was determined to start again. Just as he had done as an apprentice, he set about preparing meticulous drawings and watercolour sketches of plants and flowers, directly from life.[*1]

Significantly, he also decided to marry. He had been engaged to a young woman in 1799 but had ended the association reluctantly when she refused to join the Quakers.[*2] He launched himself into his painting and, if anything, the results were even more exciting and flamboyant than before. Yet, within a few years the old qualms and fears began to return. Haslem quotes from a series of letters which Pegg wrote to his wife from July to September 1817 when he went on a sea voyage, stopping off at various points between Bristol and Sunderland. This break had apparently been advised as a way of improving the sight in one eye which had badly deteriorated and eventually failed all together. He took the opportunity to describe how wretched he felt, which he regarded as "the punishment of disobedience" for returning to china painting and resolved to give it up again.

It was, however, three years later, in April 1820, that he ended his employment. The delay, Haslem imagines, was caused by his wife's misgivings and Pegg explicitly wrote that leaving the China Works was against the advice of all his friends. The couple took on the shop we have described earlier. Their first three years nearly ended in disaster, as, in their kind-hearted way, they gave customers credit. It reached a point where their friends had to arrange "a small subscription for my relief". The Peggs devised a brilliant solution to the problem. They would never give credit but they would be prepared to sell the smallest amounts of anything, if necessary for a farthing. The strategy was remarkably successful and they lived the rest of their lives in comfort and security – even saving 'upwards of £200' which Haslem thought well deserved the addition of an exclamation mark.

Apart from running the shop, Pegg spent these years compiling page after page of religious poetry and prose with occasional autobiographical material. His wife died in 1847 and he died four years later, aged 76, known by everyone in the area as a quiet, respected shopkeeper. The bridge over the canal opposite the shop was always referred to as 'Pegg's Bridge' (see page 35).

Haslem explains that he is able to give a very full account of Pegg's life because he has access to 'a bulky MS. Volume of Pegg's writing' which included a Journal, written in 1827[*3], an account of his life up to that point, together with a collection of letters to a friend. He adds that 'these are so mixed up with poetic pieces, essays and reflections on religious subjects, which he (Pegg) calls 'exercises', that it has been a work of time to select a few widely scattered grains of biographical fact from such a bulky and miscellaneous profusion'. Much of this bulky profusion is currently kept in the Local Studies Section of the Derby City Library. It is clear that Haslem carried out a thorough surgical operation and there is probably nothing directly related to events in Pegg's life which is not included in 'The Old Derby China Factory'. There are two handwritten books (for want of a better description) called Pegarania and Traits. Haslem does not quote from them, understandably since they are heavy reading and add little or nothing of biographical fact. However, they do tell us more about the way Pegg thought about his life and will be discussed later.

There are two things that stand out from this story which make it remarkable. One is the quality of the work Pegg produced (which will be dealt with in the final chapter) and the second is that here we have an artist /craftsman who has taken ten years to acquire a very difficult technique up to the point of perfection, whose work is applauded by those best able to judge, (his fellow craftsmen), and which has a kind of vitality that one feels must come out of the excitement of creating something good. He is a young man on the threshold of a career that could take him to the heights of his trade anywhere in the country and beyond (as Haslem demonstrated in his own London interlude). And yet, at that point he abandons it all. In our time, we can understand the tragedy of an artist who, suddenly losing inspiration and creativity, fails to produce work of the exceptional standard he previously achieved. We can easily imagine the possible effects of self-doubt, criticism, health, love-life and so on. What is virtually impossible to understand in our day and age is how someone can abruptly stop working because, for religious reasons, he believes that the whole business of decorative art is shameful and immoral. On the face of it, it is unlikely that Pegg was using his adopted religion to account for some perceived failing in his abilities, since, after apparently reconsidering his objections and returning to the factory, he immediately shows that he has retained all his old skills. After a few exercises on paper, he could resume working at the same level he had reached twelve years before.

The fact that he was known in his lifetime and subsequently as 'Quaker' Pegg is not at all misleading. To be a Quaker clearly occupied his thoughts on a daily basis and affected all his behaviour. The Quaker records show that for nearly 40 years he was the most consistent attender and the most frequently nominated representative in the Derby Meeting. All his writings concern some aspect of his religious beliefs and the autobiographical details are there to throw light on his search for spiritual enlightenment rather than to offer some kind of CV.

His involvement with the Derby Quakers is the subject of the next chapter.

FOOTNOTES

1. Haslem was no doubt unaware that a book he used for this purpose and some watercolour sketches were later given to Pegg's friend Thomas Martin Randall. In an article in Antique Collector for June 1983, John Twitchett, who was the curator of the Royal Crown Derby Museum at the time, describes the thrill of meeting a descendant of the family at an open day and subsequently acquiring this material for the Museum where it is now on permanent display. He gives a list of the contents (112 sketches) and some illustrations in his book 'Derby Porcelain ' (1980)). (See details on page 33).

2. Haslem implies that this was a personal decision by Pegg but the Quaker records of that time make it very clear that, had he gone ahead with the marriage, he would have been expelled from the Society.

3. This Journal, specifically described by Haslem, is not amongst the papers lodged in the Derby Local Studies Library and is not mentioned in the Bemrose Collection at the British Museum. I do not know whether it still exists. Probably this is not a great disadvantage since Haslem makes extensive use of it and I doubt whether he would have left out any quotation of great significance concerning Pegg's life or painting. The Traits contains something of a digest by Pegg himself of the Journal. In later chapters I have indicated which material comes from this Journal and which I have copied from the Traits.

3: Pegg and the Derby Quakers

As far as Pegg was concerned, 1800 was the most significant year of his life. In 1849, two years before his death, he wrote a kind of autobiography and this was its full title: "Traits of the Singular Life of that Persecuted Man for his obedience to the Truth, Wm. Pegg who joined the Society of the People called Quakers in the year A.L. 1800. Understandeth What thou Readest".

To have some idea of what this meant to him and his contemporaries, it is necessary to give a brief summary of the history of the Society of Friends, both nationally and locally, up to the point when he joined. Derby and the surrounding area featured prominently in the very earliest years of its development in the mid 17th century. The story of those years told by the founder, George Fox, in his Journal seemed far too good to ignore (after all, the title of Quaker itself was coined by a Derby Magistrate) and is covered in the Appendix, together with a more detailed history of the Society in national and local terms, for those who might be interested.

The history of the Society of Friends begins in 1647 when George Fox started out on a career of nomadic preaching which he sustained for over 40 years, making his way through every English county several times and not only into Wales, Scotland and Ireland but also Holland, Germany, the West Indies and America. He began this mission in the midst of the turmoil of the Civil War and acted as a catalyst, bringing together large numbers of individuals who rejected the authority of the established Church as well as the monarchy. The rejection was comprehensive; not only did it object to the clergy, established religious procedures and buildings but also to virtually all the creative arts: music, dance, theatre, painting, fashion, and non-scriptural literature. It regarded these as, at worst, idolatrous and, at best, unnecessary distractions.

Understandably, such a drastic challenge to the existing order was resisted by the authorities and Quakers were frequently before the courts, imprisoned and punished. After the Restoration of the monarchy under Charles II, they were targeted by specific legislation. It says something about human nature that these years marked the highest number of professed members (possibly for all time in this country). Many legislative measures were rescinded by the end of the century and numbers declined, partly through emigration mainly to North America. This decline continued throughout the 18th century when no Quaker took up Fox's form of aggressive proselytising. This was left to John Wesley with equally spectacular results.

However, Fox had initiated a structure which developed into Monthly, Quarterly and Annual Meetings attended by representatives of local groups which has held the Society together ever since. These local groups were now called Meetings too, where attendance for religious observance, perhaps best described as discussions, was usually on a weekly basis. Anyone could be present at these gatherings[*1] but anyone wishing to become a committed Member of the Society had to undergo a strict vetting procedure and adhere to severe standards of behaviour which, as we shall see later in this chapter, were applied to Pegg. This meant that, while numbers might have declined, the Quakers became a very distinctive group as far as the rest of the community was concerned. They usually dressed in a different way. Their objections to some issues were met by a regular system of payments for exemptions. They were excluded from parliament and the professions which meant that many channelled their energies into trade where their honest reputation meant that they were trusted and often prospered. The century saw the development of Quaker projects in education, provision for the impoverished, the abolition of the slave trade and improvements in the treatment of prisoners.

On the local front, after Fox's whirlwind missions in the earliest years, activity was concentrated within limited areas in Derbyshire, mainly around Moneyash and Chesterfield. Derby itself was dormant but was surrounded by Meetings in Nottingham and Castle Donington outside the county and by Furnace and Breach ten miles and more to the north-east of the town.[*2]

Breach was originally called White-lee and the first recorded reference to it was in 1673 when 10 shillings was raised to pay for transport to the London Meeting. The Meeting-house was rebuilt in 1693 and it continued to secure substantial attendances in the 18th century – Watkins estimated 200 to 300. When Pegg came to Derby in 1795 and took an interest in Quaker beliefs, this is where he had to go. He records in his Journal: "I attended a week-day Meeting about the space of a year, and because there was not a Meeting-house belonging to the Society in Derby I went to Breach meeting about 9 miles (from Derby)". We can assume that he walked there and back.

Pegg had arrived in the town just at the time when things were beginning to stir. As he goes on to explain: "A room was at length fitted up in an old mill in Derby for a Meeting-place and it was opened as a place of worship on the 18th of the third month 1800, which was the first day of the week" (the Quakers refused to adopt normal names for days and months because of their pagan associations) "and it was the first meeting for worship that was settled in Derby belonging to the Society of Friends but it was too small to hold public meetings in, and Derby, being frequently visited by Ministering friends, it was thought best to build a Meeting-house large enough. This was done in the year 1808".

The initiative came from members of Breach, under the general jurisdiction of the Nottingham Meeting. Pegg and three others were the first applicants to be new members of the new Derby group. It is a guess but it may explain why he made this choice, after hitherto attending Calvinist and then Baptist services, since presumably it contained a set of lively young people who had drive and plans. He remarked that, as a child, he had listened to a sermon given by an elderly John Wesley and found it uninspiring.

The subscription list for the new Meeting-house, which is still today the centre for Derby Quakers, shows that he contributed five shillings. Some others donated as much as £40 and the total raised locally and nationally came to £1100. His was the lowest amount but, at a time when he was scraping a living as a stocking-knitter, probably represented a valued part of a hard earned income.

We can have some idea of the success achieved by the Derby Meeting from a report by a visitor, Henry Hall, in 1810. "Until lately Friends had not a meeting settled in this place but several being convinced have joined the Society and a good meeting house is now erected in which we had two meetings, the last very crowded, several hundred not being able to get in".

Earlier, I have tried to explain that there was a distinction between those who might attend meetings and those who became Members of the Society of Friends. These Members had to be able to persuade the Meeting (that is the local group) that they had genuine 'convincement' and that they kept to standards of morality in every aspect of their everyday life. Once a Member, any individual could be expelled from the Meeting if they subsequently failed to maintain these standards. How this was applied and what these standards were, can be best demonstrated by giving the details of Pegg's involvement in the Derby Meeting throughout his life, as recorded in the Quaker archive.

The report on him by the interviewing committee dated 13th of the tenth month 1799 was as follows: "William Pegg hath attended the meeting house here for a considerable time past, appearing to be thoroughly convinced of our religious principles and we believe zealously engaged to walk consistently therewith, and we refer his case to be considered with the rest previous to our next Quarterly Meeting."

At the next meeting on 12th of the twelfth month 1799: "We feel it easy to recommend Jonathan Oldham to be admitted into membership with us and thought it at least safe for the applications of the others to remain under consideration till another Quarterly Meeting and in the meantime to be under the care and notice of Friends and of this committee".

A fortnight later Jonathan Oldham is admitted but they hesitated over the others though "no improper discouragement might take place from its being a little longer delayed". At last on 24th of the third month,"we have had separate conferences with (the three remaining applicants) and on said consideration thereof, we think it may be most safe to recommend to the Quarterly Meeting to receive all of them into membership."

Incidentally, we can note that the interviewing panel on 20th of the sixth month 1802 records: "The said Friends had an opportunity with Ann Hedley who hath attended our meetings about two years: she appeared in a tender frame of mind and gave us an account of her convincement and reasons for joining our Society in a manner that excited our sympathy and appearing to claim the regard of Friends towards her and we propose that her case may remain for further consideration". She is approved for Membership on 15th of the eleventh month1802.

Whenever a Member moved from one area to live in another, as Pegg did in 1806 when he moved to Hinckley, subsequently to Bedworth, to Coventry and back to Derby in 1813, the Meetings had to provide references for each other. For example, the Middle Monthly Meeting for Warwickshire on the 3rd of the eleventh month 1813 wrote: "William Pegg a member of this meeting being removed into the compass of yours we hereby certify that he was in good esteem here and that we believe his conduct was in a good degree consistent with his profession some enquiry has been made and nothing appears but that he is free from Debt and Marriage Engagements amongst us. We hereby recommend him to your friendly regard and oversight and are with love Your Friends" (Signed by five names).

This provision of, so to speak, certificates of good conduct may not be confined to Quakers. The first letter in the Derby archive is dated 13 November 1796 and is from the pastor at Hanley to assure Derby brethren that William Pegg is 'worthy of communion with you'. Interestingly, it actually reads 'as requested a full dismission from us to full communion with you' but the writer has inserted 'he has' between 'as' and 'requested' – possibly insignificant but also possibly an addition required by Pegg after reading it, since perhaps such a 'dismission' is not a normal formality at all.

This brings us neatly to how Friends were expected to conduct themselves. It is possible to see this in some detail by considering the papers kept in the Quaker archive which refer to various individuals called to account for their misdemeanours. The list for Nottinghamshire and Derbyshire during the first half of the 19th century, the period Pegg was a member, includes the following: 'For leaving his mistress before the end of his term of apprenticeship', 'Drunkenness', 'Fornication', 'Debt', 'Non-attendance', 'Not being sufficiently guarded in his conduct', 'Marrying outside the Society', 'Insolvency (and drunkenness)', 'Failure to fulfil his engagements', 'Aiding and abetting her daughter to rob a bank' (actually, this involved forgery rather than anything more dramatic), 'For being married by a priest', 'Immoral conduct prior to their marriage'. If the case for the prosecution was proved, the penalty was "to disown them as members of our religious society".

Evidence was collected when appointed Friends visited and questioned the accused and this was submitted to the Monthly Meeting. Within three years of his return to Derby, Pegg was allocated to make such a report and again in subsequent years. In fact, from 1814 onwards his name crops up year after year fulfilling various duties from door-keeping to reporting on the library and acting as representative at Monthly Meetings. Indeed he is a representative every year, except 1848, until appointed for the last time on 28th April 1850, a year and eight months before his death. In the fourth and fifth month of 1847 he signs a report that preparatory meetings were not held 'for want of attendance'. Perhaps, as attendances flagged, he was one of the few remaining activists. (The Derby Meeting's attendance return for the 1851 national survey, for the day appointed, was 42 in the morning and 30 in the afternoon). Although I was not able to compare directly the handwriting between the minute books held in Nottingham and Pegg's manuscripts in Derby, I suspect that some of the minute books were in his hand.

There is also a poignant detail in the minutes from1847; on 21st November "Wm. Pegg reports that himself and Wm. White attend the monthly meeting. A burial note for Ann Pegg wife of Wm. Pegg with Registrar's certificate is brought in which the Representative is determined (?) to take to the monthly meeting to be held in Nottingham and be approved."

As can be seen in the earlier paragraph, control over the conduct of Members was particularly applied in relation to marriage. The following declarations had to be made before Ann Hedley could be approved as a wife for William Pegg.

Derby 21st of the fourth month 1814

This is to certify that it is with my consent that William Pegg proceed to take my daughter in Marriage.

Signed Ann Hedley (with a cross)

Witness Thom Hedley Thomas Pegge

Castle Donington 29th of the fifth month 1814

To Friends of the Nottingham Meeting

Dear Friends,

We have made the needful inquiry respecting Ann Hedley and do not find but she is clear of marriage engagements excepting that of her friend William Pegg.

We are your good friends

Elizabeth Young Sarah Ellis

As a committed Friend, Pegg went through all these procedures but it should not be thought that he regarded them simply as formalities. In the Derby papers is a series of letters written by him in1829 concerning the predicament of his cousin Sarah. She had been engaged to a William Hutchinson and he had broken it off 'quite without her consent'. Pegg writes to a senior Quaker: 'It is therefore proper that she should be recompensed, if this were proved in a court of judiciature she would be entitled to half of his property. She has the power of appealing to the monthly Meeting for redress...the sooner this is done, the sooner her mind will be relieved from the grief that she is labouring under and the sooner will tranquillity be restored amongst us. If you decline to do this, the deficient answers to the queries will bring it into the Monthly Meetings. Thy Friend William Pegg.

NB. Tho her grief is new every morning, yet she says 'don't say anything to him to hurt him'. While we are endeavouring to love mercy, it is our duty to do justly and it becomes us to walk humbly with God."

Later that month he writes to William Hutchinson and becomes involved in the charge and counter-charge common in such situations. "Several things rest on my mind – one is the charge thou broughtest against my cozen in these words "She told me a story to turn me against my daughter" thou art thinking of clearing thyself of her without her consent by charging her with something – the charge here brought is false, so she says, and it appears to me that thou could not possibly know her motive for the alleged story to wit that it was to turn thee against thy daughter. She says she never thought of such a thing as turning thee against thy daughter. I want thee to understand that I see through thy deceit and am with love thy friend desiring thou mayest repent. W. Pegg"

The documents in the archive give no indication of what happened next.

All this goes to show how encased Pegg was by his Quaker membership. Although this was mostly prescribed, it was his deliberate choice and, as I shall attempt to show later, he chose to interpret it in its more rigid form. It was essentially the Derby membership too. It is clear that in Hinckley, Bedworth and Coventry he did not feel he had the same strength of support as he gained from Friends in Derby. He seems to have kept up a very regular correspondence with at least one of them while he was away. An entry in the Quaker records suggests that in 1821 when he was setting up his shop, he adopted a sort of pawning arrangement with them for a table. At his time of need, when he was falling into debt (grounds for exclusion from membership), they assisted him financially. There is no evidence to support this but I would like to think that the strategy, which you may remember he subsequently adopted in the shop, no credit but no purchase too small, was part of the rescue package. After all, many, if not most, of the Quakers were in business and would be capable of offering experienced advice to a novice. It seems too that he developed the enterprise. The 1829 directory has him down as 'Grocer, Baker and Dealer in Flour' (although in later editions he reverts to being a simple 'Shopkeeper'). Perhaps he was influenced by his old friend, John Steer, the recipient and preserver of his letters, who had apparently discovered the value of diversification. He had been a needle-maker but in the same directory is described as 'Umbrella and parasol manufacturer, optician and toyman'.

It is not easy to tell from Haslem's account, how much support he also drew from his old workmates at Derby China. However, his shop was literally a stone's throw from the factory and it would be hard to believe that workers there were not regular customers. It might also be worth considering the relationship he had with Haslem. Of course, there was a large age difference, Pegg was 33 years older, but, on the other hand, they had been very close neighbours for 13 years and you might have expected them to have had much in common to discuss and for Haslem to use in later years. Yet it seems clear that Haslem draws practically all his information from documents. It might simply have been a taboo subject. But we are left with the impression of Pegg as someone with a profusely passionate inner life which he spills into his writings, while everyone else sees a quiet, withdrawn, probably unsociable, personality.

When he was not spending his time earning a living and attending to his commitments to the Society, he seems to have devoted much of his remaining energy to composing tracts, possibly to deliver at the Meeting-house, with some poetry and, especially in the final years, after his wife had died, long-winded surveys of existence in general, his life and world history, all overwhelmingly informed by his religious convictions. This makes up a substantial part of the archive. In addition there are the letters he wrote between 1806 and his return to Derby in 1813 and then a group of letters he wrote to his wife when he went on the sea trip from Bristol to Newcastle in 1817. Apart from using some of these documents, Haslem quotes at length from the 1827 Journal. The next chapter will attempt to describe all this material and select extracts from it to try to learn, from his own words, a bit more about what he was like, how he lived his life and the decisions he made.

Footnotes

1. In the 1851 Census to ascertain the exact extent of religious attendances throughout all denominations, the statistics were based on the average attendance over a short period and the number of seats available – except for the Quakers. It was agreed that they should assess theirs by the amount of existing floor space. Only the Quakers and the Unitarians did not require payment to rent some of their seats.

2. Furnace has a Meeting House and a burial ground which can still be seen, opposite the Amber Hotel on the road between Oakerthorpe and Higham. Traces of Breach have disappeared except for one small patch of white plaster on a barn wall and the piece of land where it stood is partly overgrown with brambles. The Quaker archive contains a copy of a lengthy delightful handwritten account by Ernest Watkins, a Fritchley Quaker, of his efforts in 1909 to find, for his own satisfaction, the exact location of the Breach Meeting House and Kidsley Park ('On the Track of Old Friends in Derbyshire'). Kidsley Park, a farm, was twice mentioned by Fox in his Journal –in 1650 "many were convinced in Kidsley Park" and in 1654 "And then I passed towards Kidsley Park, where there were a-many Ranters came: but the Lord's power stopped them". The farm still exists, close to Heanor Gate School. The records show that the farming family living there in the 19th century continued to be Quaker Members.

Watkins investigated by means of day-long expeditions on foot, giving step by step details, including conversations with whomever he chanced to meet on the way. Ultimately, while searching for Breach, when it was starting to get dark and snow was falling, he arrived at a farm on the corner of Breach Road and Codnor-Denby Lane. With the help of the friendly farmer and his ladder, Watkins was able to look at the patch of white plaster on the barn wall, all that was left of the Meeting House demolished in 1834. Today it looks exactly the same as Watkins described 100 years ago. It was replaced by a Meeting House at Heanor, also confusingly called Breach, mainly through the initiative of the Howitt family.

4: "Such an Inclination for Writing"

Any outline of the origins of the Society of Friends has to rely mainly on George Fox's Journal. This is of necessity because it is the most detailed and accessible account. It is also attractively written, at times entertaining, always vigorous, and he incorporates into the narrative extensive assertions of his faith which he apparently delivered in public at the time. Without doubt, this Journal was a model for Pegg both in content and style.

Indeed, it has to be said that, by accident or design, Fox's life seems like a kind of template for much of Pegg's development. When Pegg found his circumstances in Derby unbearable (mainly it seems because of his mother; 'the hard language and ill treatment she has practised on me'), he chose to move to Hinckley, only four miles or so from Fox's birthplace, where, as far as we know, he had no relatives or friends. Both married relatively late in life and had no children. Fox and Pegg were the same age when they decided to write their Journals.

Yet, for all this, it is quite obvious from their everyday behaviour that Fox and Pegg were totally different personalities. Fox was a forceful, restless, dynamic extrovert. Pegg was a mild-mannered introvert. Both were prepared to resist conventions but whereas Fox would openly condemn others, Pegg would usually quietly agonise on his own. Although unassuming in his daily life, he was precisely the opposite in his literary activity. His fervour was channelled into his writing and, to be suggested later, into his painting. As he put it: "I have such an inclination for writing, I can scarce satisfy myself".

His writings in the archive date from 1806 until 1850, the penultimate year of his life. They consist of letters, poetry, biblical tracts and a surge of material completed in the final years, probably after the death of his wife, where he attempted to consolidate the beliefs, opinions and experiences of a life-time, as comprehensively as possible. To give a fair picture of what writings he left behind – and indeed, almost certainly wanted to leave behind – it is necessary to divide these elements up under separate headings. It should be stressed that the sheer volume of the material devoted to each section by Pegg himself bears little relationship to the relative importance we would give it. Modern interest (or at least mine) focuses on the narrative of his life, the explanation behind what we would regard as an extraordinary decision suddenly to abandon practising a supreme skill on moral grounds and on the actual products of that skill. Pegg's interest is overwhelmingly concerned with his religious ideas, expressed in poetry as well as prose. The account he gives of his life, which is usually given in some detail in any modern reference to him, takes up a minute portion of his output and even this is heavily interlarded with biblical comment and interpretation. The letters, apart from those to his wife, were presumably preserved by the recipient, John Steer, and none of Steer's replies survive. Apart from a few references to "lust of the eye", nothing is said about his painting. Given our agenda, the poetry can be disposed of fairly briefly but must be mentioned since it clearly meant a lot to him.

The Poetry

Pegg wrote to his friend in 1808: "There are rules for making poetry…as I don't intend to be a poet, I don't think it worth while to perfect myself in them, and the more so, as I am not a proper grammarian. And this is my sentiment of such poetry that it's nothing less than marred prose". Despite this, he wrote a lot of poems throughout his life. It must be said that they are mainly doggerel and hardly deserve repeating. His hymns are a bit better. One of them appears in John Murdoch and John Twitchett's 'Painters and the Derby China Works' Catalogue (1987), as printed in the Bemrose Collection. Here are a couple more:

Son of Righteousness arise,
Fringe the curtains of the skies
Chase away the gloomy night
Welcome lovely morning light.

From the yellow glowing east
To the glowing azure west
Shed thy softest purple beams
Tinge the pools and flowing streams.

Gild the towering stately rocks
Warm the little bleating flocks
At the feet of lofty hills
Guard them safe among the rills.

Come thou holy wind and blow
O'er the verdant plain below
Blow upon my garden ground
Shed the purple dew around.

In the radiated bow
Permanent thy promise show
Send thy servants forth to dress
Nature's barren wilderness.

In each season of the year
Let its proper fruits appear
May the first and finest be
Dedicated unto thee.

Mighty power that made the sun
Speak the word and be it done
Fire thy people's length of days
Hearts and mouths to sing thy praise.

. . . . .

Praying at thy holy feet
Unregarded shall I lie
Never say it is not meet
Father hear a sinner's cry.

Weak, I am a captive bound
Save me from the tempter's snare
Set my feet on holy ground
Lay me low and keep me there.

These might pass muster with many Hymns Ancient and Modern – which, of course, doesn't say too much for them.

The Letters

The letters mainly come from two periods of his life. The first group covers the years from 1806 to 1812 when he was away from Derby. The second is a series he wrote to his wife when he was on the voyage around the coast in 1817. There are a few letters and numerous tracts from his later years. Haslem quotes extensively from the first two groups. I will try to select extracts that throw particular light on his personality and the way he struggled to run his life in accordance with his religious convictions.

1806 to 1812

At first Pegg enjoys the relief from leaving Derby or perhaps more precisely a nagging mother. He writes to her from Hinckley: "I enjoy better health I think than I have done of many years". "I wish thee to make thyself agreeable and sociable amongst Friends and I hope they will be so toward thee and in particular John. (John Steer, the recipient of most of these letters) I believe it will have a tendency for good, from thy affectionate son. WP."

He goes to London to see whether he could make his living there and writes excited letters describing his adventures. "I had not thought there was such a place in the world. I compare it to a city in a Paradise". Before long, however, he realises that a move there is not a viable proposition and he is stuck with Hinckley.

On his way back he uses the experience to reinforce the decision to give up painting. "I think I am in a state preferable to my former one, when I earned my living in those things which had their rise in the lust of the eye and the pride of life: and when I saw this to be so, I could not boast (as to that) a conscience void of offence between God and man". In another letter around the same time he seems to be answering those friends in Derby who are trying to dissuade him from leaving: "Remember Lot's wife. No man having set his hand on the plough and looking back is fit for the kingdom of heaven. Would friends in Derby defile their hands in this delicate traffic were it not for the mammon which they scrape together thereby if they could find it easier a path without it. I trow not." He elaborates –"I judge it wiser to wear a coarser coat and to have a smaller income than to launch out into purple and scarlet and fine linen trades, it would become us more in the sight of God and man for it is a certain truth that if we love the world the love of the father is not in us. And by the way, I may observe that friends of all professions wear the finest clothes but to leave this subject".

At the end of the letter he obviously thinks he has gone a bit too far and John, the correspondent, who is a needle-maker, might imagine he is being criticised. "And after giving my opinion, I may as a friend be allowed to give my advice, which is this, keep that thou hast if thou art not inclined to make more sacrifices, give not back the things thou hast attained. Give my love to thy sister and to all other friends and to my mother when thou seest her". This seems to me a wonderful strategy – state your opinion and then 'as a friend' give advice which more or less disregards it.

There is a fervour in the earliest letters, a 'hell fire' touch, which though never far away, is rather more muted later on. "We are called to come out of Babylon that great city which is full of costly delicacies and abundance of riches for the inhabitants within her walls. Love her she is called the mother of harlots and of abominations of the earth. In her was found the blood of the prophets. Our espousal to Christ is as a marriage". "I am escap'd as a bird from the net of the fowler – I was as a vessel of the Lord in the house of Baal. I stood in the gain of oppression and the superfluity of naughtyness was my daily employ having had my eyes opened. I saw it right to flee from the wrath to come – in the moment of the divine requiring – obeying that glorious call, come out of Babylon Oh my people! In affection, Your fd. William Pegg.

It is interesting to see here where Pegg is marshalling all the arguments for abandoning his trade, that he calls it the 'gain of oppression'. In a letter from Hinckley the following year, he writes: 'I am no friend of oppression – the people of Hinckley are very ignorant and consequently very incredulous – one may also make them believe anything – that is the effect of poverty they are kept down'.

It is clear that, while he is convinced that he was right to leave Derby and all that entailed, minor irritations turn into major physical and mental suffering. His Quaker background cannot have helped much, with its deliberate attempt to distance itself from the frivolities and social niceties which most of the rest of the community rely on to get them through the week and to signal this not only by conduct but also outward appearance. “The neighbours in the yard are said to be ‘a rum lot’, and in particular the women”. “One may enjoy such retirement without being interrupted with the foolish and unmeaning expressions of ‘How do you do?’ ‘Good morning!’ ‘Good night’ etc. etc.” (This is in fact a precept which appears in Fox’s Journal and presumably not much help in his later role as a shopkeeper). It should be noted that when Pegg refers to ‘retirement’ he means silent meditation or contemplation. He often found walking alone in the countryside particularly inspirational.

In a further letter to his mother, who no doubt wonders why on earth he has to maintain this irrational position, he writes: ”I do want to live at Derby again but it does not seem likely at present – conscience is work that Christians profess to obey and if I am not found in this obedience I shall be found to be a hypocrite. Woe to you hypocrites – it will be better for Sodom and Gomorrah.. I am derided by some, it is not without a cause. I do indeed think myself foolish but it’s faith that hath brought me to it …if any man will be <u>wise</u> let him become a <u>fool</u> that he may be wise.”

In April 1806 he reflects on the fresh insights his new circumstances have given him. “There is no better preservation from temptation, as to out ward, than to be kept bare of money.” “I saw many things amongst friends in the course of my journey (walking near Derby on a visit) which I should have looked on with an eye of indifference some time back but which now appears like superfluity or luxury – shows(?) a great deal of difference between the thoughts of those who <u>abound</u> and that it is hard to learn how to abound without being lifted up (I mean proud) as it is to learn how to want without being in despair”.

By 1808 he is learning that idealising the benefits of poverty has its limits and he has to draw very heavily on his faith to survive physically and mentally. The tone of his letters changes. Two years earlier he had signed off a letter “Your sometime suffering and sometimes rejoicing friend and brother”, by now there was not much rejoicing. “I have had the scurvy about my eyes at times for some years but last autumn being worse than usual, was obliged to have recourse to outward assistance, my eyes became pretty much cured but the disorder not being inwardly cured, broke out in each wrist violently and with working my wrist bands and the sleeves chafed the places which caused a constant running that weakened my arms so much that the cold has taken hold of them and they are now in such a state that I have no prospect of doing much in the frame at present. This would not trouble me but have not enough of my own to keep me with till I may be better." If the diagnosis of scurvy is correct, presumably it arises from being unable to afford sufficient suitable food or indeed sufficient food of any sort.

If he had to draw on his faith, he also, to his shame, had to call on his friends but they were in Derby not Hinckley –"having none on whom to depend and being in a state not fully able to work. I have nevertheless been endeavouring to feel after a state of calm resignation yet when I reflect that my income falls short of my outgoings it has no pleasing effect on my mind for I fear if I suffer myself to shrink into debt without a prospect of discharging such debt in due time this will unavoidably bring me into disgrace. I am obliged to thee for the assistance thou hast handed me but I cannot think of being thus time after time assisted – it is time thou begun to think of thyself. I have never worked with my frame with pleasure since it was renovated". He goes on to complain about the poor accommodation he is obliged to work in and the cold but "what has hurt my feelings most is the want of sympathy of some about me…my income has been so small during the winter that at times it has given a great deal of pensive thoughts and at times sorrow has taken deep hold of me – I had much better income last summer before I came here and before my frame was done and now I am weak of body and dull of mind. I am not able to work with that spirit that I have done neither is my time my own so for as to use it for my advantage. Thus have I told my melancholy tale."

This seems to have been his lowest point in the letters. A month later he writes: "I am in a stouter state of body than when at Derby last and the ulcers on my extremities are healing except my wrists. As to spirituals I think I have been more favoured of late than of some former periods, have seen afresh the necessity of standing prepared for the great and awful change of the body the consideration of which leads to a disentanglement from the things of this world and throws a shade over all the joys. The reflection on these subjects has relieved me from some anxiety concerning future and uncertain days." Pegg has indeed learned 'how to want without being in despair' but rather typically by contemplating mortality.

Thankfully, he changes his lodgings and "I am in good health and fatter than I have been in years". However, it is doubtful whether he ever felt comfortable in Hinckley or Bedworth and one suspects that this is to do with the local Friends compared with those he left behind in Derby. Without making the point explicitly, who else can he mean when he writes: "There is a little danger amongst enemies that you see and a great deal of danger amongst those who lay concealed about you"? When "two friends who are overseers in the Monthly Meetings submitted the matter to my consideration whether I had not better leave the place", he takes the hint and moves to Bedworth. One can surmise that this was because he was not regarded for personal reasons as "one of us" but it seems to me much more likely to be a reflection of his persistent financial problems. In fact, in a letter to Steer at this time, he confesses that 'I borrowed the money that I sent to thee'. We have already noted how a failure to maintain financial security is sufficient to exclude someone from a Meeting. At Bedworth and Coventry, reading between the lines, these problems were not solved and probably were responsible for the unpleasant experiences he had at the Meeting in 1812. "It was visited by Thos. Shillitoe, and also by Stephen Grellet under whose Ministry I suffered much".

At this point, letters to Steer in the archive cease. There is only one letter in the collection from Coventry and that is not from Pegg but to him from a Mr. Cash: "..when it was mentioned to me of thy moving thy seat it hurt me much. For why should one seat be considered better than another?"

It would have been enlightening to read letters written at the time he decided to return to Derby, especially as there have been so many with such detail from the previous five years. We might wonder why none appear. It is always possible, of course, that letters were written and, for any number of reasons, have not survived. However, I think that Pegg provides the explanation in the Journal; he fell even deeper into depression. Clinical depression results in inertia. The effort of writing letters and even of shaving would be too much. The account he gives in the Journal is graphic enough to be quoted in full.

"I seemed to have lost all I ever knew about religion. I was even on the verge of Despair! and not only given up to the buffetings of Satan, but the Fire arose in my bosom to that degree that I was already in the Bottomless pit; and until this time I did not know that there was such a state to pass through, neither could I at that time see the end of it.

I could not take my rest in the night season, and my appetite fail'd me, so that I began to wear away, and all persons that came near me were dip'd with a feeling of my condition, so that I was ashamed before all. I said surely this cannot be the Lord's work? But I had forgotten what the Lord's Mission was! "He shall baptize you with the Holy Ghost and with fire" and "The chaff shall be burnt with unquenshable fire!" At this time of sleepless nights, I arose out of my bed frequently in the night season, and walk'd about the room covered over with a Rug.

I often walked out for retirement in unfrequented places. During this time I wore my beard. I was not shaved within the year from the time that I neglected to do it…My mind was disturb'd with unpleasant dreams in the night season and 'the candle being lighted in Jerusalem', for under this figure I describe the state of mind in the daytime, this I found to be close searching of the heart; I was made willing to sacrifice anything to obtain Peace. No one knows what it is to pass through the valley of the shadow of Death but those who have experienced it."

For the actual moment of conversion or as he put it, 'the fiery trial which is to try every man,' we have a more detailed account in the Traits.

"If any man's work be burnt, he shall suffer loss. But he himself shall be saved yet so as by fire – 1st Corinthians (iii)'
Our friend used to walk for retirement behind the city wall near the hole where the Bishop of that city was burnt for the testament of Jesus that he bore, but the fire was of Divine origin and designed to purify the soul from all those things that were combustible or burnable nature. Now the fulfilment of the testimony of holy writ was verified in his experience – and in ardent prayer among the wild brambles of an old and deserted brickyard, the Almighty was pleased to hear his prayer, and then it was that the water of the Holy Spirit quenshed the burning flames that fired his breast."

And off he went, back to Derby, back to ceramic painting and into matrimony

Details of Illustrations

DM&AG: Derby Museum and Art Gallery (Museum number in brackets)
RCDM: Royal Crown Derby Museum

34. Thistle Dish 1800. No mark. DM&AG (1884-166/62)

35. Pegg's Bridge. Photographed in 1963 by Derby Borough Police shortly before its demolition. The building beyond in the lower photo still exists on the corner of Robert Street and is on the site of the Derby Porcelain Factory. www.picturethepast.org.uk

36. One of the courts almost next to the Peggs' shop. Photographs taken in 2010.

37. Plate 1796 - 1800. See Twitchett (2002) p. 310. Plate Book 240. Described as 'flowers by Peg'. Blue mark. Private Collection.

38. Flowers with caterpillars and Portrait. 1813. Mrs. Joan Shaw.

39. Convulvulus minor. Sketchbook 1813. RCDM.

40. Tulips. Sketchbook 1813. RCDM.

41. Tulip and moth. Sketchbook 1813. RCDM.

42. Chrysanthanum and tulips. Sketchbook 1813. RCDM.

43. Plate 1813-20. Gold border. Named flowers: Martagon Lily, Wood Nightshade, Monkshood. Red mark. DM&AG (1904-376/45).

44. Plate 1813-20. Gold border. Named flowers: Rose of Heaven, Yellow Martagon Lily, Anemone and Borage. Red mark. DM&AG (1904-376/47).

45. Beetle. Sketchbook 1813. RCDM.

46. Dish. 1813-20. Gilt edge. Named flowers: Peony, Great Honey Flower, Viper Buglass. Red mark. DM&AG (1904-376/82).

47. Cake Dish. 1813-20. Named flowers: Chilwell Rose, Eastern Poppy. On reverse: Nasturtium, Anemone, Convulvulus Minor and Tulips. Red mark. DM&AG (1904-376/88).

48. Detail of Thistle Dish c.1813 and preparatory sketch 1813. RCDM.

49. Plate. 1813-20. Gold border. Named flowers: Great Bluebottle, Mountain Primula and Rose Cestris. Red mark. DM&AG (1904-37649).

50. Reverse of previous plate.

51. Plate.1813-20. Feather. Gold mark. Private Collection.

52. Dessert plate. 1813-20. Named flower. Esculent Poppy. Red mark. DM&AG (1928-157/21)

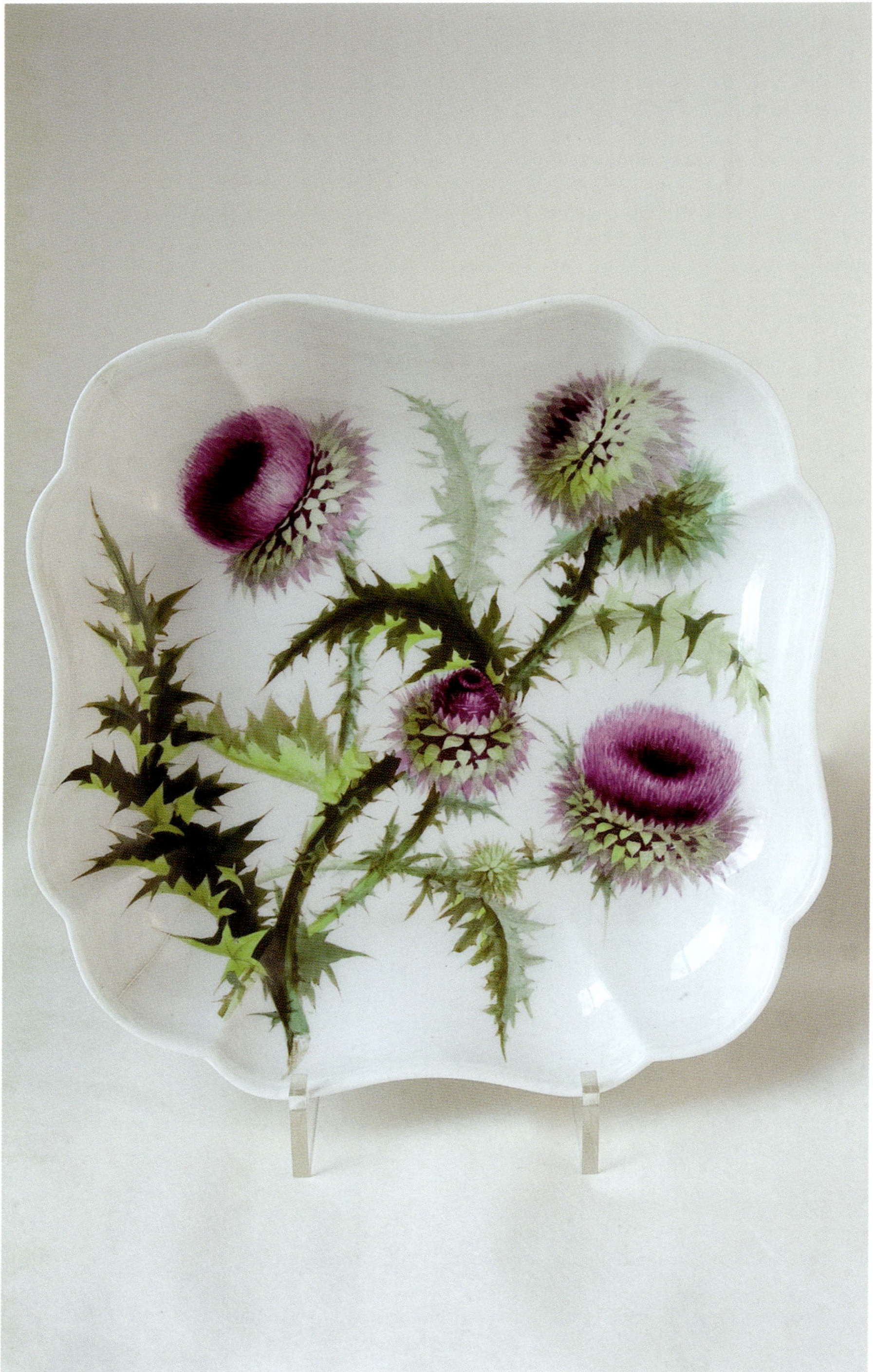

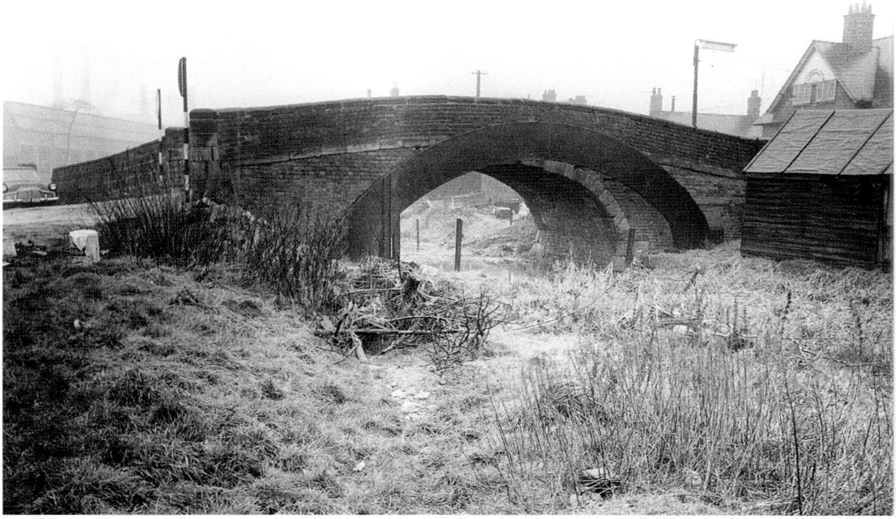

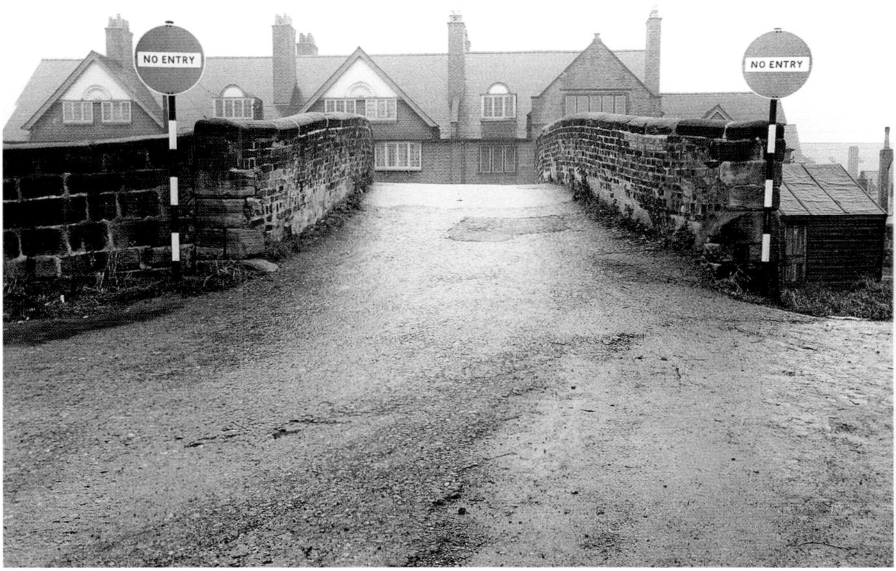
NO ENTRY
NO ENTRY

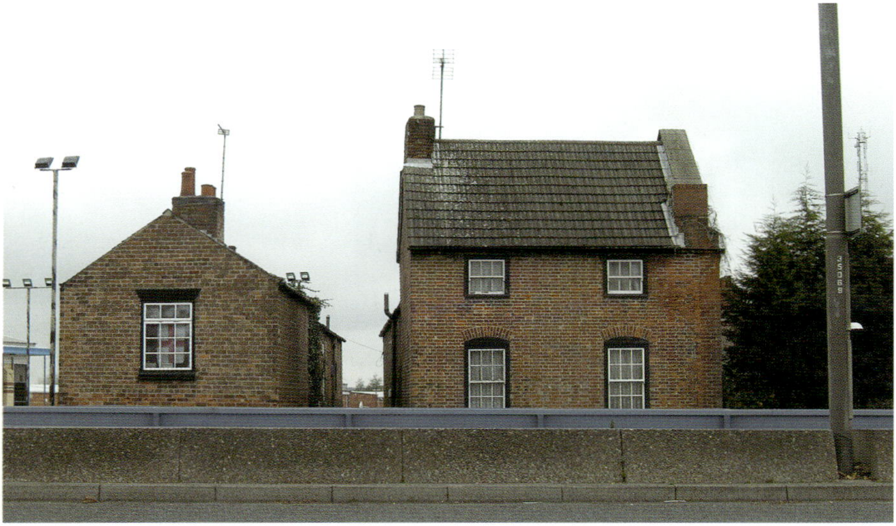

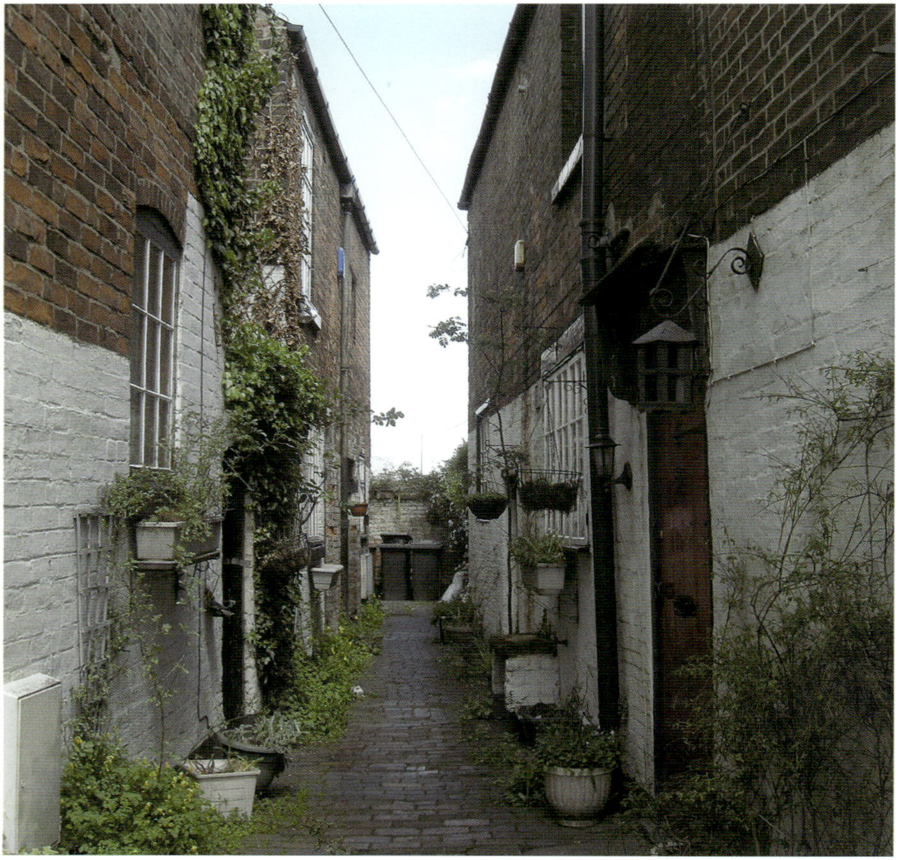

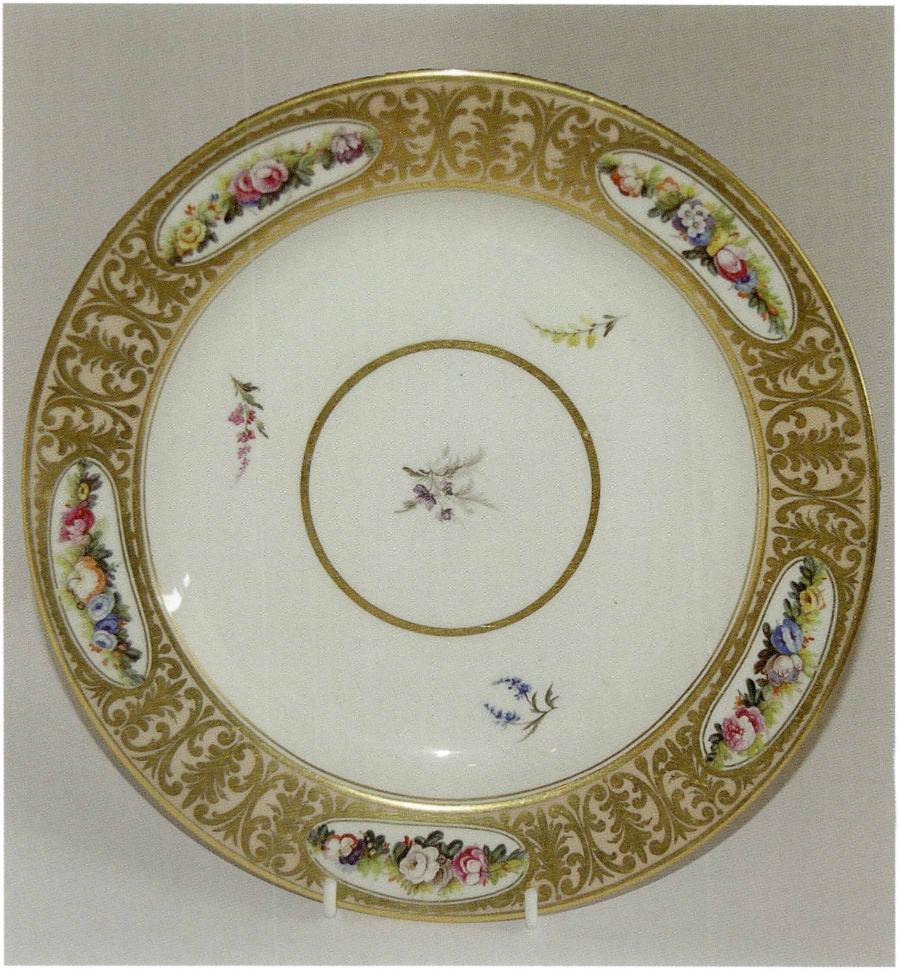

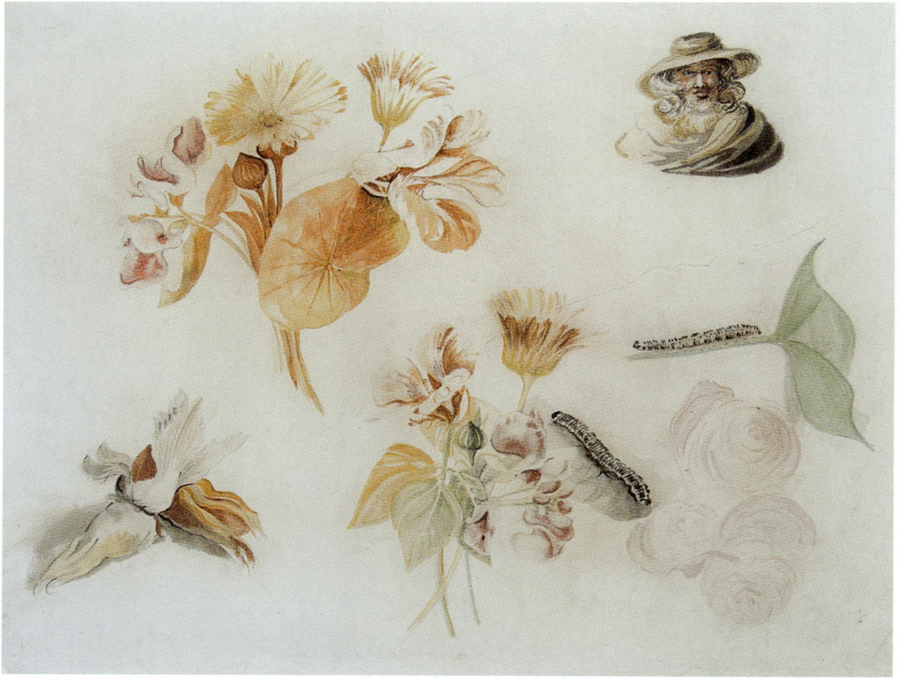

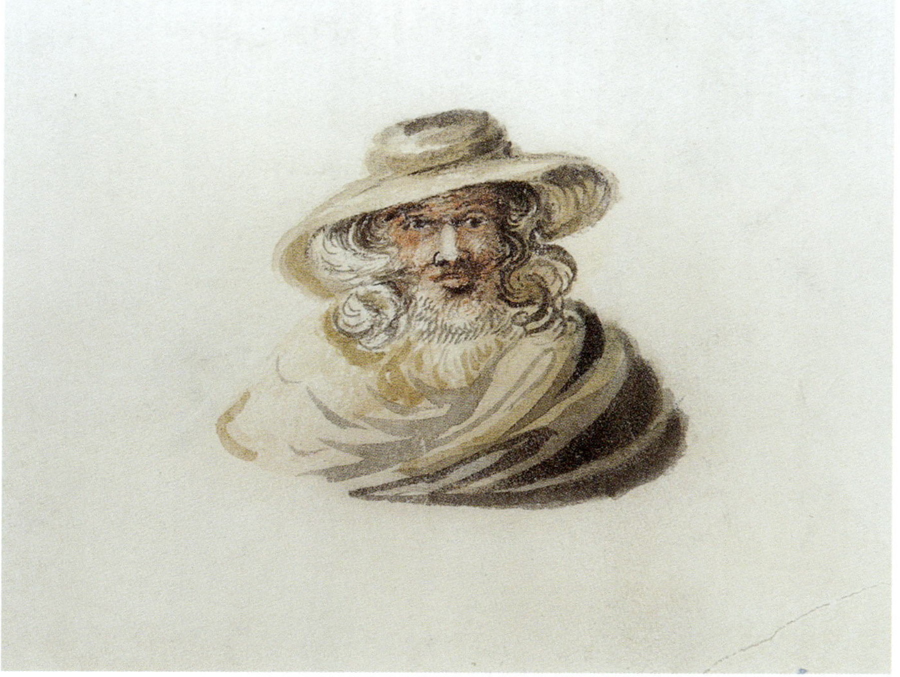

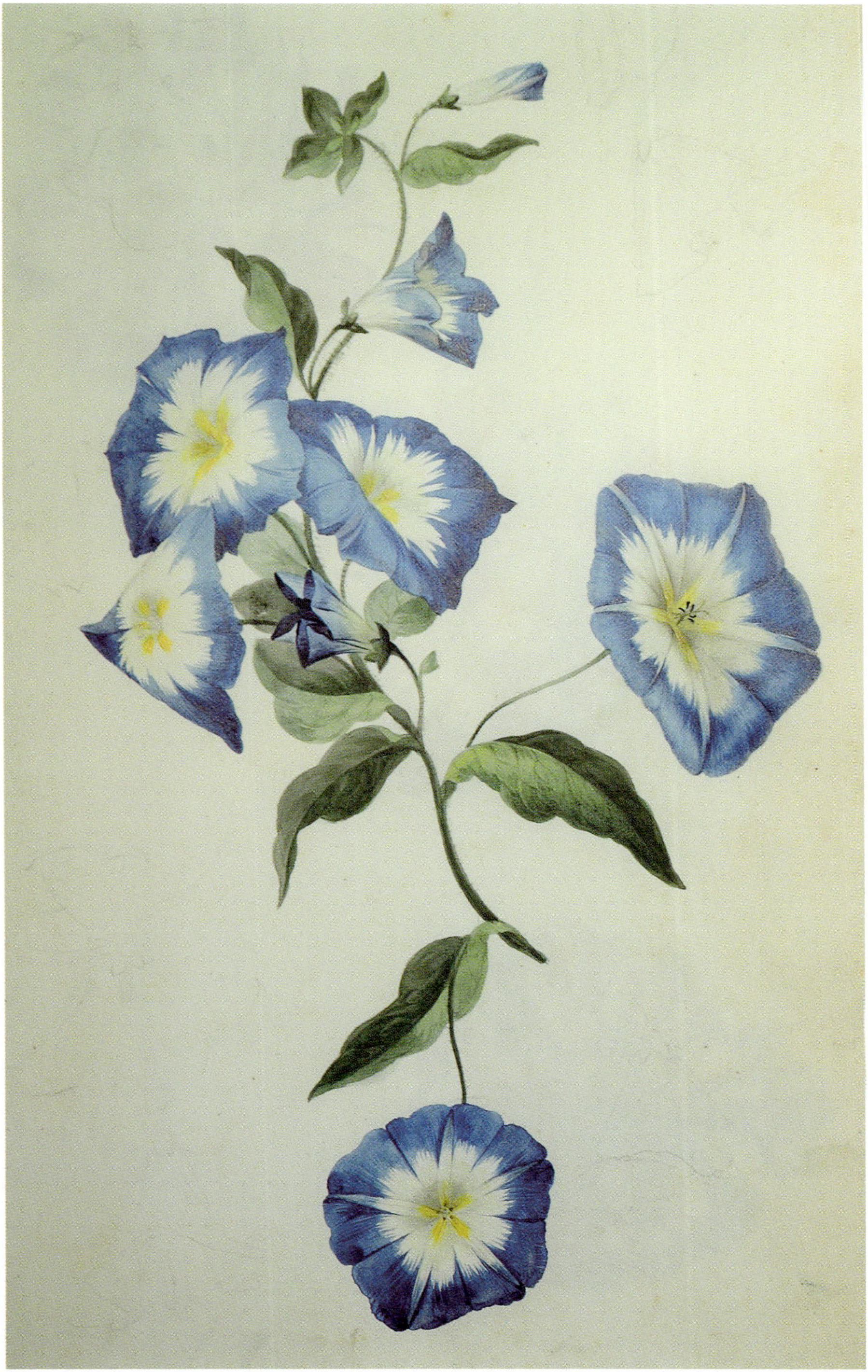

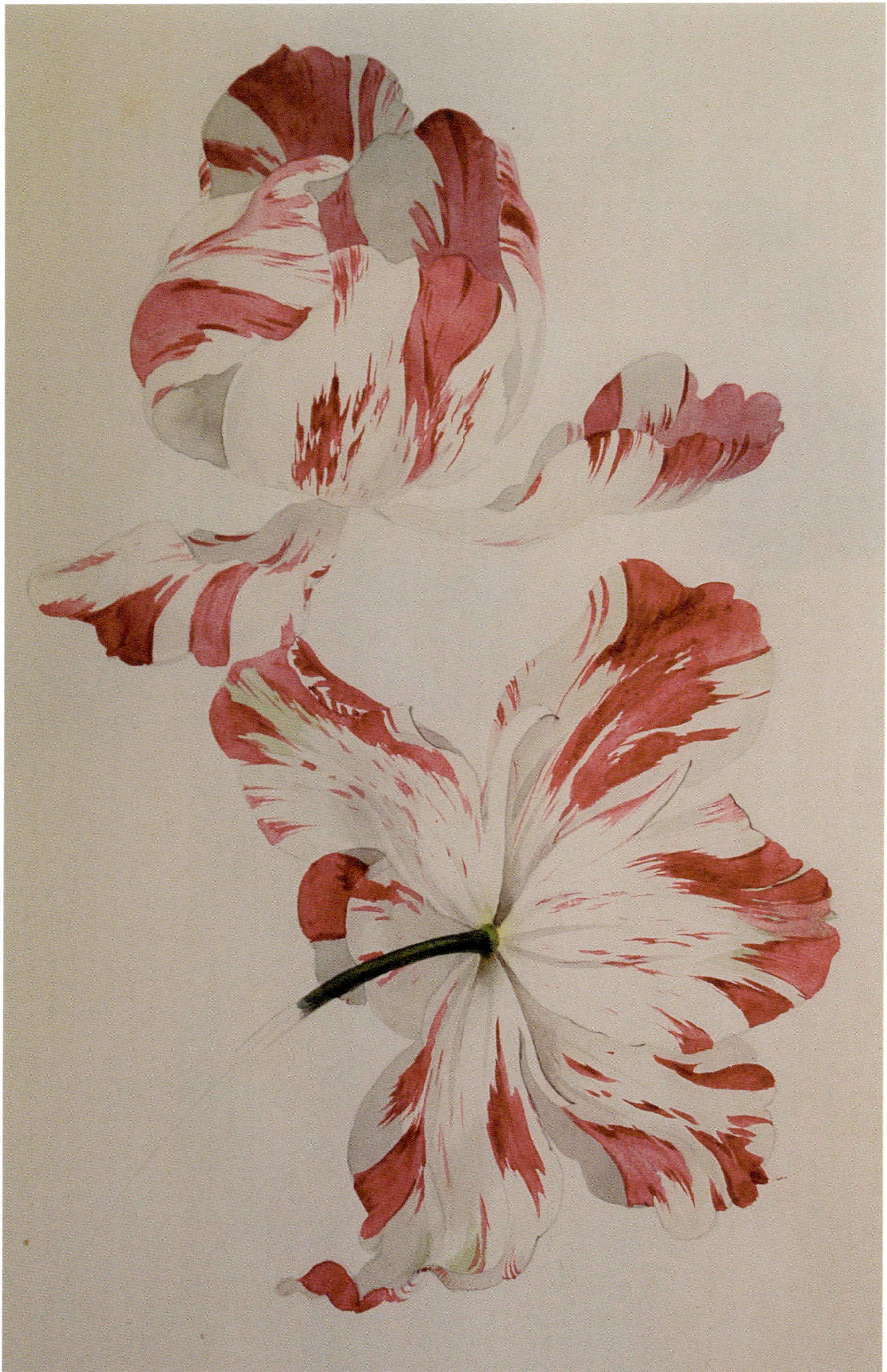

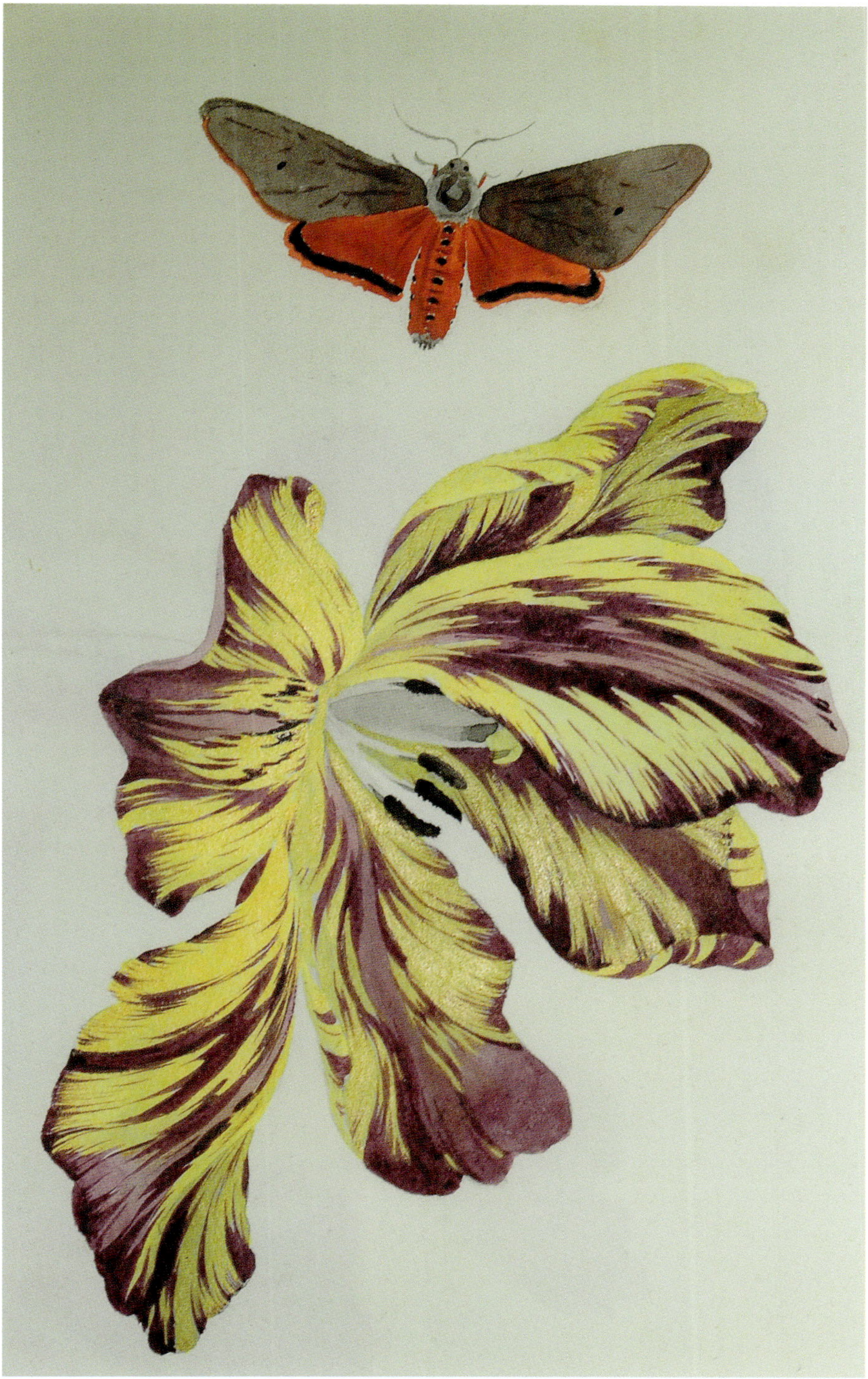

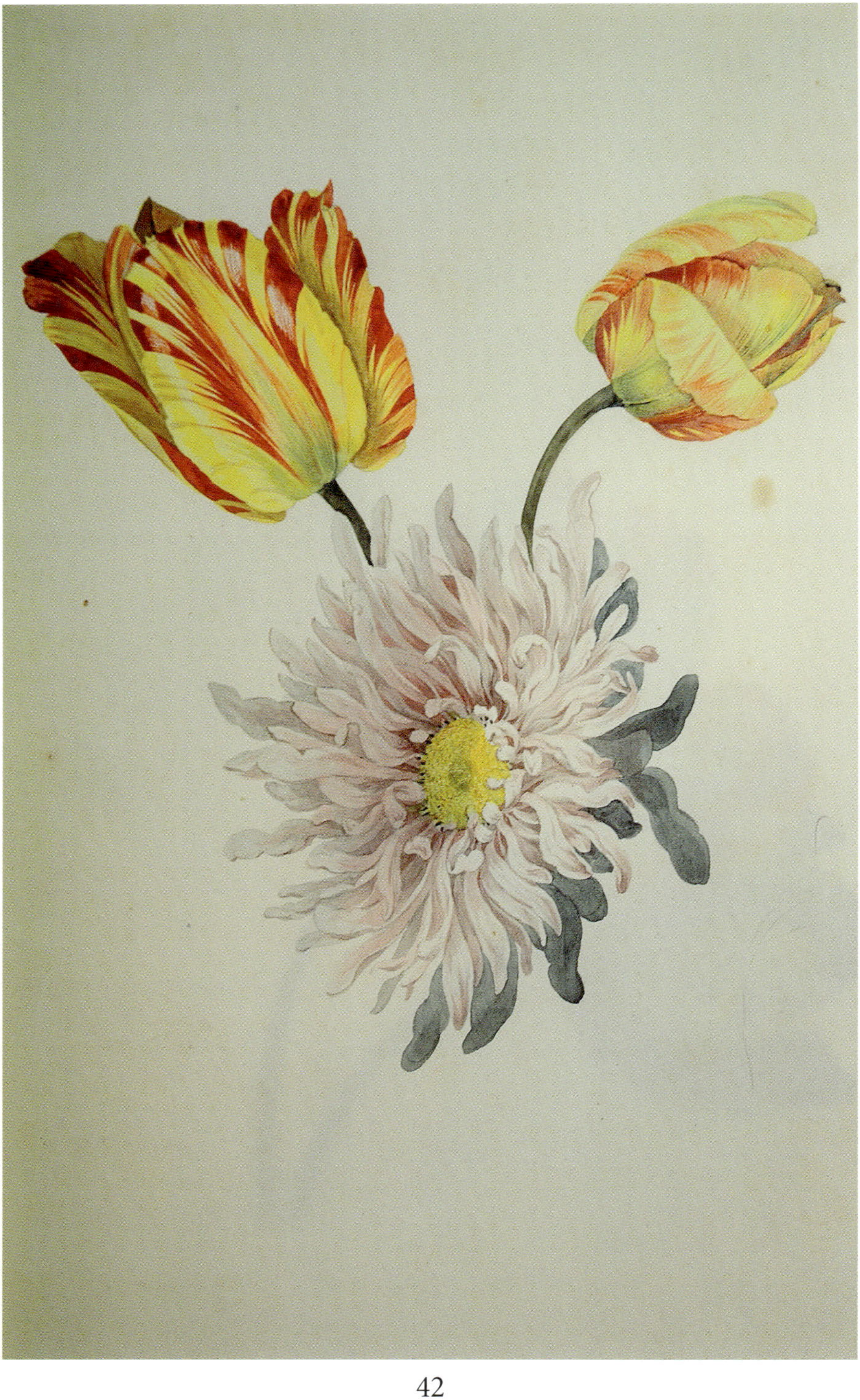

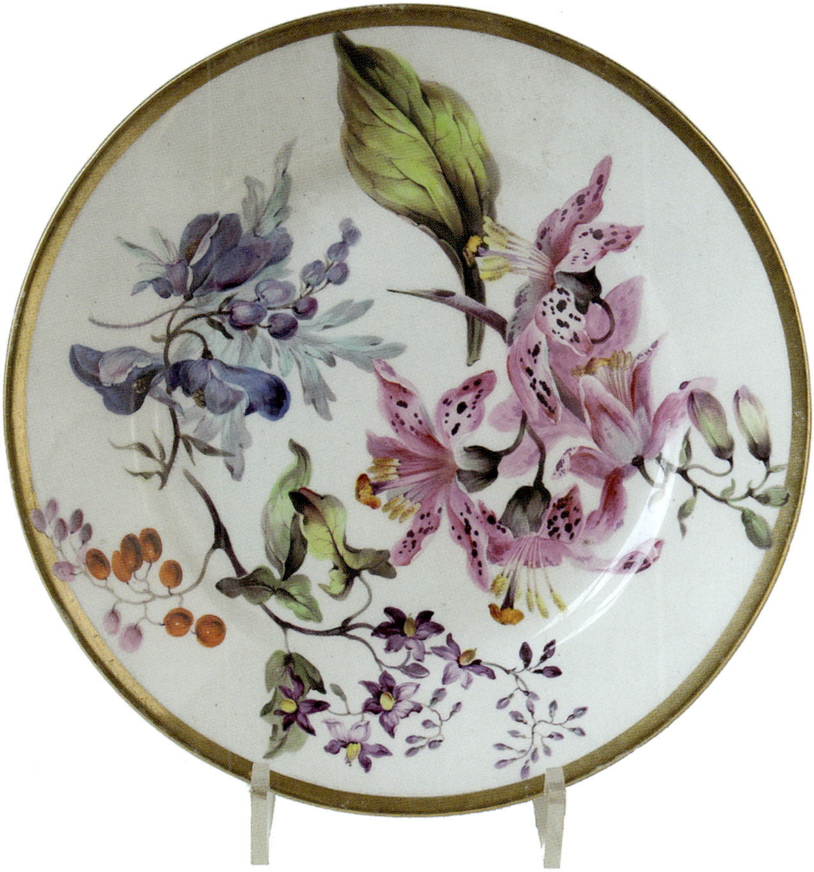

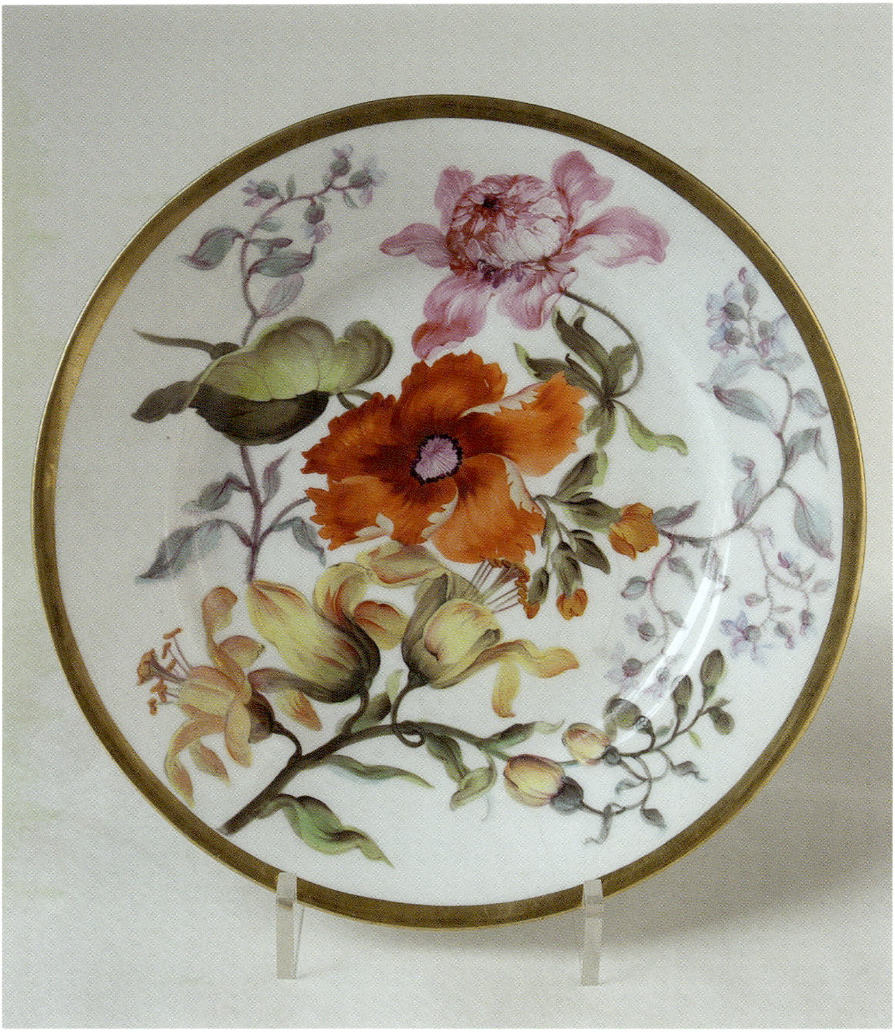

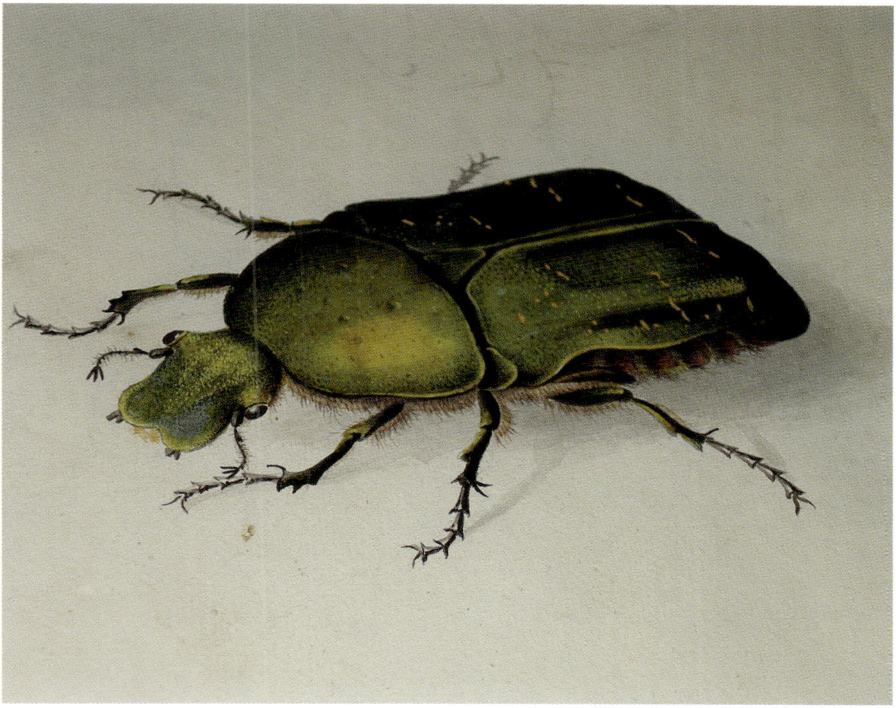

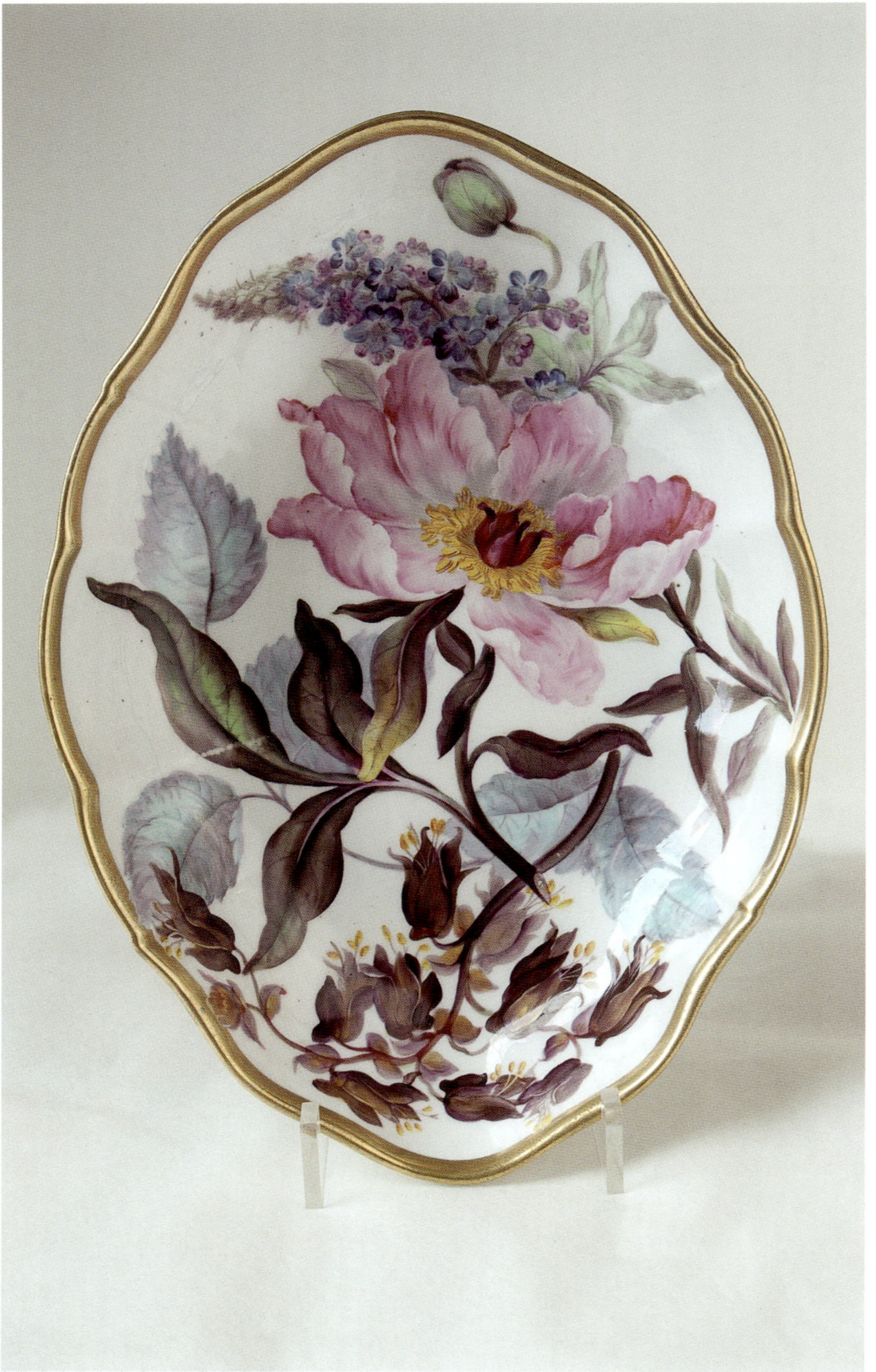

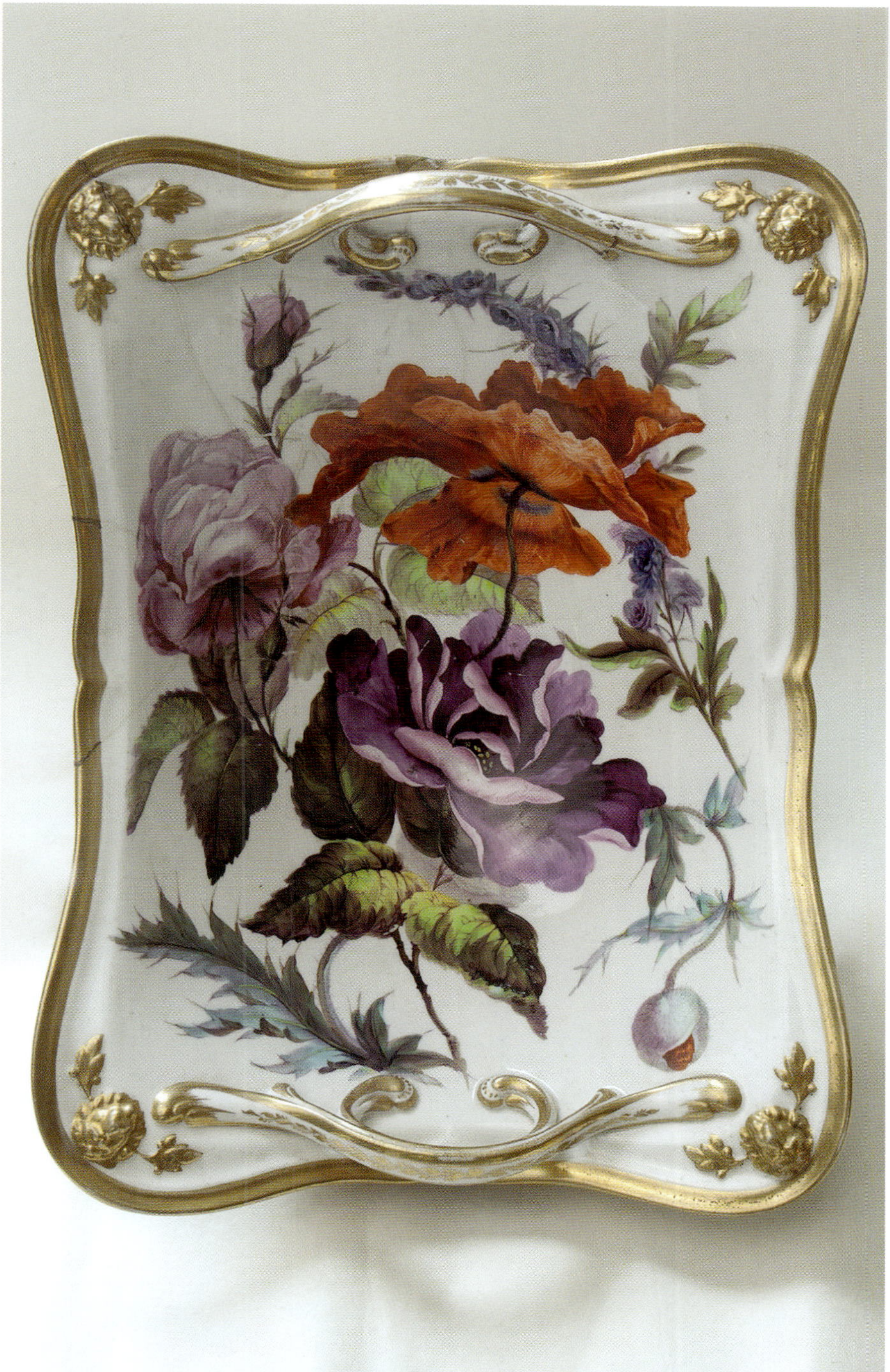

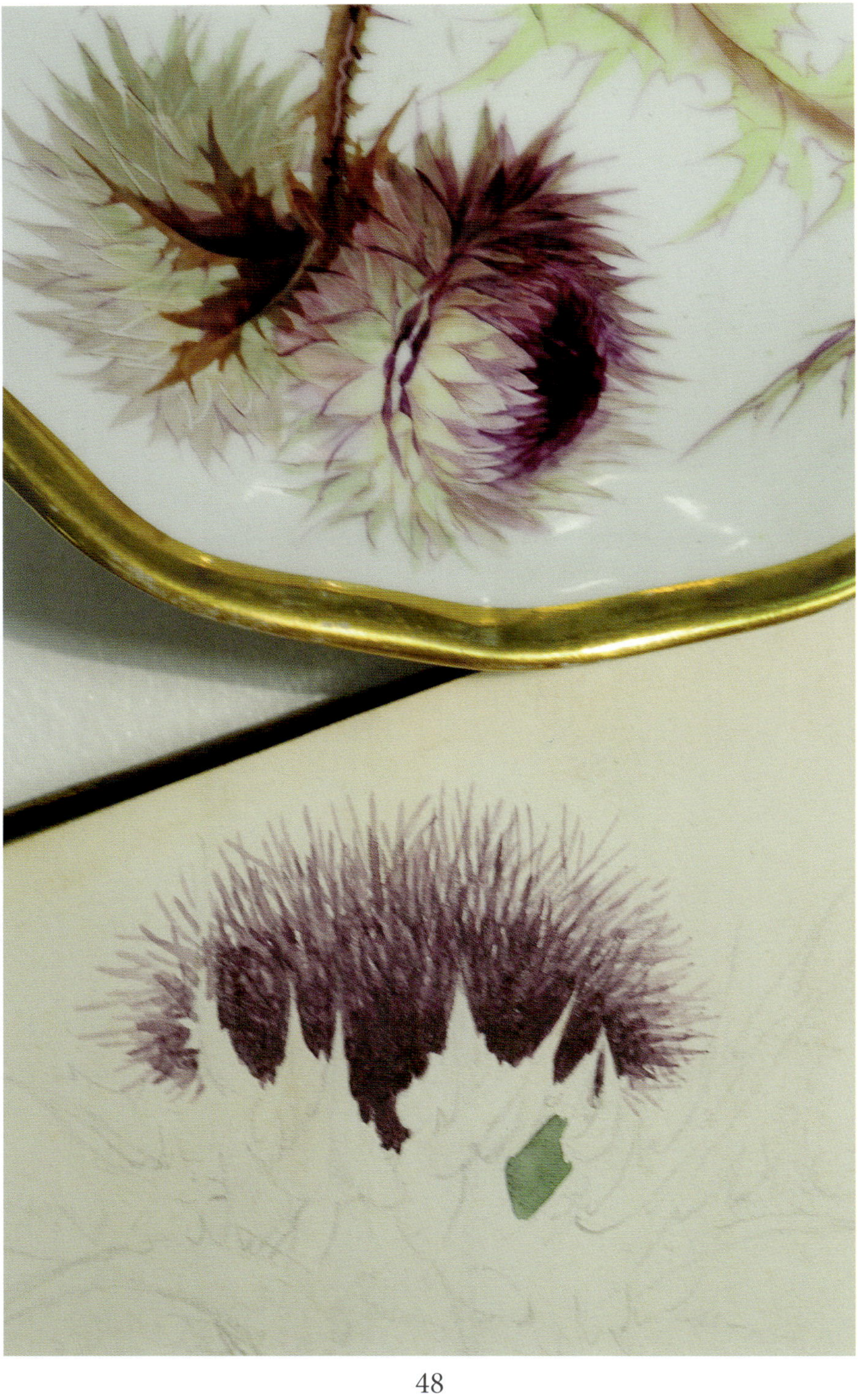

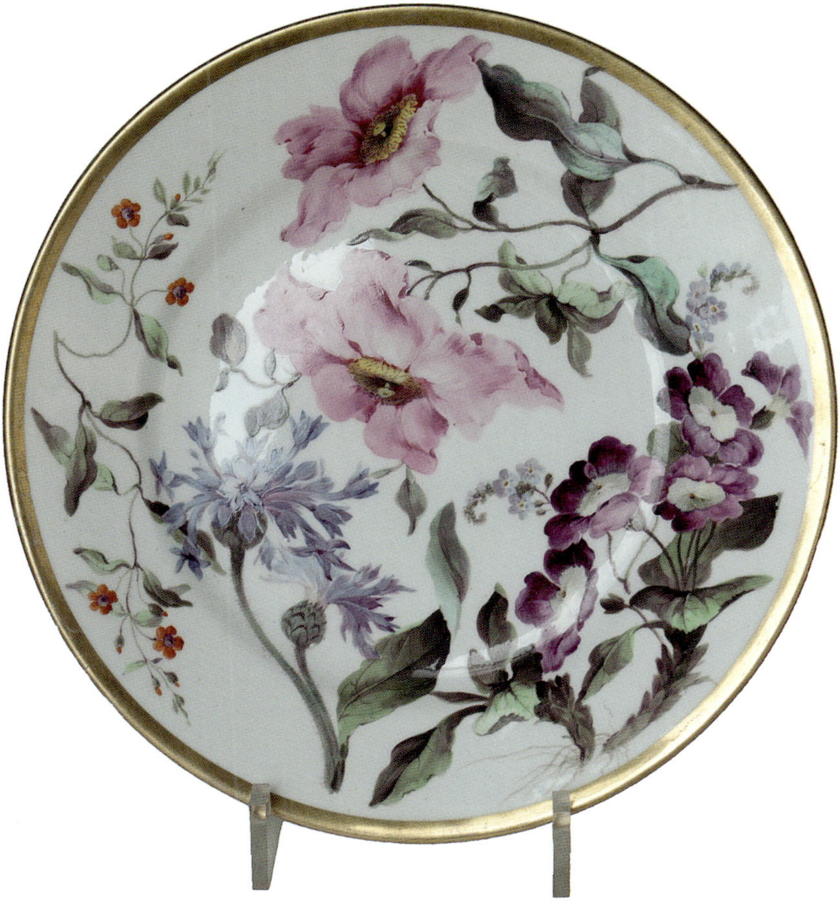

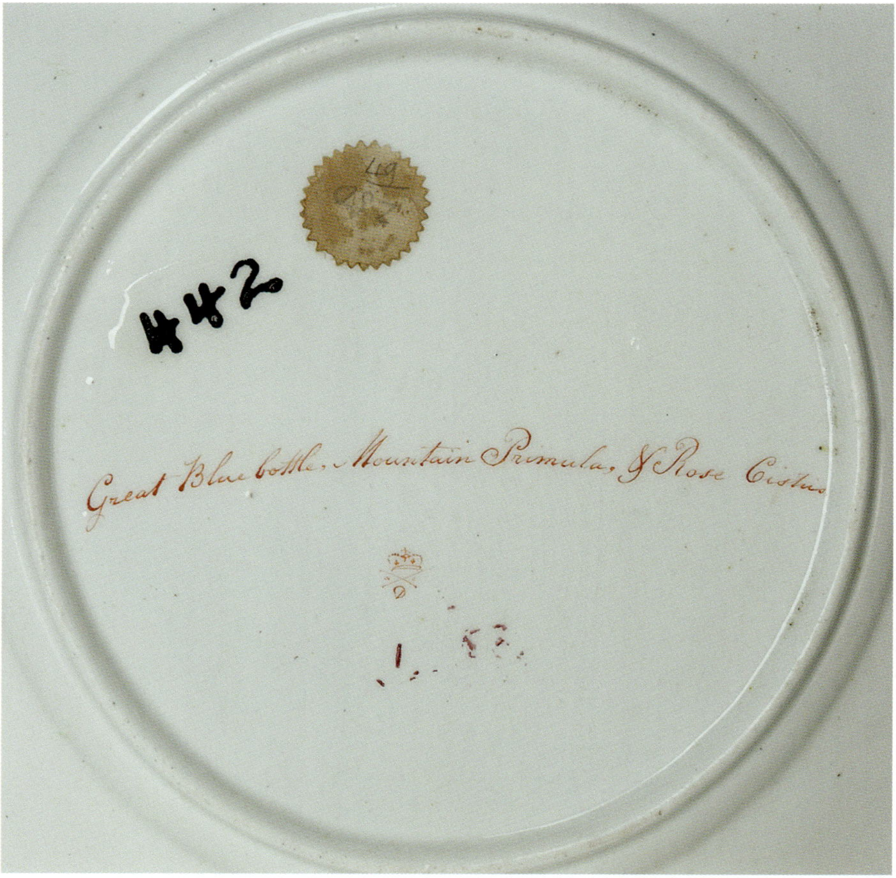
442
Great Blue bottle, Mountain Primula, & Rose Cistus

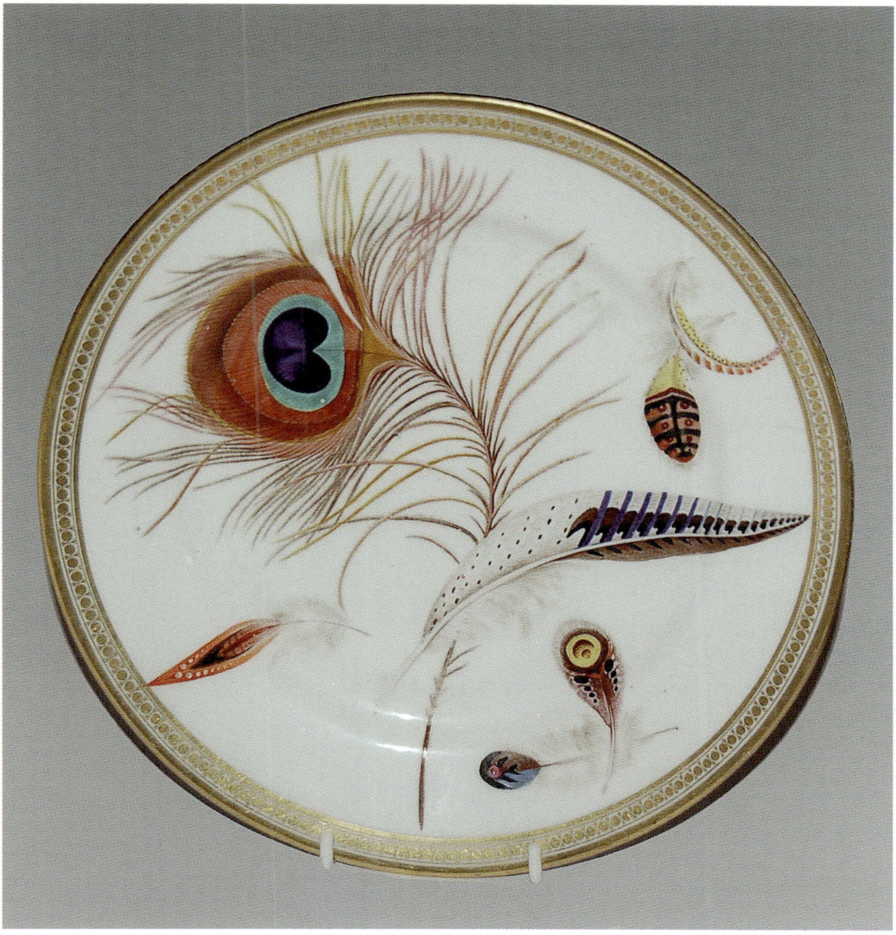

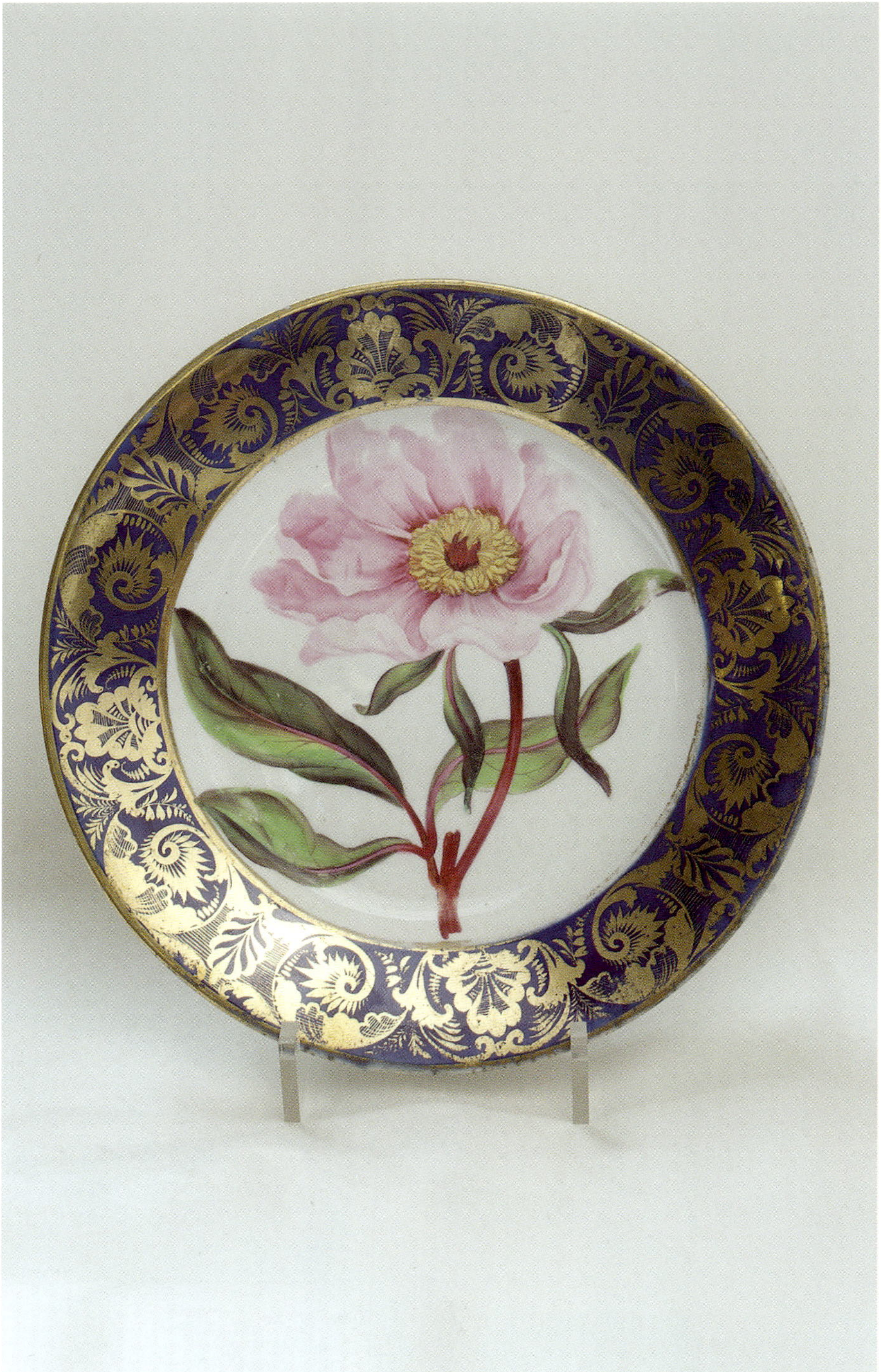

The 1817 Voyage

The group of letters that Pegg wrote to his wife in 1817 are worth quoting at some length because they give particular insight into the relationship he had with his wife, his misgivings about his employment and the tortured way he continued to struggle with himself.

In a letter dated 9th of the fifth month 1817 (now in the archive but apparently not available to Haslem) while he was on an errand delivering papers over a mortgage from his employer, Mr. Bloor, to a factor in Newcastle on Tyne, he writes: 'Dear Wife, In hope that thou art in health and long to be with thee. I have no other wish than that we spend the remaining part of our lives together comfortably – I think I am better in health as to my bodily feelings but with regard to my eyes I am not without my fears'.

However, three months later his 'bodily feelings' seem to have deteriorated and he goes on a trip to the north east, embarking at Bristol on a cargo boat to try to sort himself out and probably to see whether a break from painting improves his eyesight.

He sends a letter from Swansea on 6th of the eighth month 1817: 'I found some improvement in my eye since I have been here, I now do wish I could take myself to some other business for a living which if I do not, I feel too sure that my peace of mind is broken. I have long felt, and have been inwardly convinced, that I was acting contrary to what was required of me, in taking to and continuing in the China business. I know, and I often feel the Divine monitor at work, but I have not had strength to say this much to thee before, neither do I suppose thou has suspected such a thing, yet for want of this sympathetic feeling we could not be united as we otherwise should have been – true love consists in acting in unison with each other in all cases and conditions and I feared if I told thee what my feelings were, thou wouldst altogether disapprove of it, this I have been suffering in my inward feelings a long time…Some others have proved themselves very kind, but I often think friends make more free to say these things to me when I am in low circumstances than they would at other times. I mean such things as are apt to hurt the mind which in addition already wounded and in a degree of melancholy seems to cut the deeper and wound the feelings more. I have

none to open my mind to but thee – here I end my epistle in weeping. W. Pegg'
As a postscript he added 'Better not write to me again'.

She probably didn't write but on 3rd of September he sends a letter from Hull, "My condition proves the uncertainty of terrestrial enjoyments. We were comfortable and happy none more so as to outward things, but I always had a feeling of mind only known to myself, and which, till of late, I could not impart even to thee. Thou will forgive me for telling the truth. In all probability I had not attempted the voyage if thou hads't acquiesc'd with me in my feelings and desire above hinted at."

A fortnight later he had reached Sunderland and was saying that he felt much better. He has enough confidence to launch into a passionate account of his dilemma and the solution he has reached. "I have suffered much in my mind of the disease called melancholy, both night and day… I have remembered there was a time when I was in the severe exercise of Religion, but that was when I endeavoured to be faithful to what I saw to be a duty required of me alas that time once fled away. Thanks to the goodness of the Almighty he left me not to perish in my rebellion…He led me into the valley of the shadow of death where I was punished with fire and fiends and hardness of soul and darkness (let no one dispute this) or if I may express myself in other words, I was broken in pieces and spoil'd, this is the circumstance that might never be forgotten. Then it was that I saw Jesus to be precious, then I felt an interest in the dying sacrifice who suffered the cross for me. O the punishment of disobedience! The dagger pierced heart, the whip beaten back, the face burning with confusion, the upbraiding of Satan. These things I cannot describe so as to make thee feelingly understand what I mean but these things I have passed through. This was a deathly baptism. Now I feel to want a life of conformity with God – to his requirings – to be what he would have me to be, no longer halting as it were between two opinions. Thou mayest remember what was said to one formerly 'Go and sin no more lest a worse thing come upon thee'. As I have been baptised into death so I want to experience a resurrection into life – I do already feel feel the comforts of goodlyness but I want thee to feel a share in my sufferings and in my joy. I know a few words from thee might – would – operate either way, it is in thy power in a great measure to make me either happy or miserable hereafter.

I leave these things before thee for thy serious consideration with my sincere prayers for thy present and eternal welfare. I remain (my dearest Ann) thy affectionate husband WP.

The days in ports, waiting for the ship to discharge cargo, he mainly spent walking alone on the sea shore, gazing out at the sea, much as he would have contemplated the countryside during his frequent solitary walks around Derby. Indeed, he might even have found it a less distracting environment. In a very typical self censure, he wrote in the Traits: ..“but walking does not answer fully the desired end and purpose, both the eye and the ear are amused with the objects that take their attention, so that retirement is interrupted continually.”

We may wonder what immediate effect these letters had on his wife. By the sound of it, they could very well have arrived like bombshells though she must have been aware of his earlier history and was possibly sensitive enough to realise that not only his eyesight troubled him. The euphoric tone may, from one point of view, denote a mystical spiritual experience or, from another, a tendency towards a bi-polar disorder. If the latter were the case, I cannot somehow imagine that Mrs. Pegg questioned his mental health. I think she would have accepted his interpretation. She was apparently a committed Quaker and had remained so independently for over twelve years before he came back from Coventry and into the picture. Subsequent events suggest that her most likely response was to tell him to take his time and prepare sensibly for a future outside the China Factory. If he was bi-polar, there does not seem to be evidence that episodes broke out again, except perhaps in 1827, until after her death when he poured out the Pegarania, the Traits and the rest. She clearly acted as a stable influence and whatever else these emotional letters display, they show the great respect and affection he had for her. He obviously saw theirs as an equal partnership and in this, as in other aspects of his life, he fails to conform to the stereotype we may have of the Victorian husband. As Haslem put it: “Take them for all in all, probably a more quiet, harmless, and well meaning pair never lived than William Pegg and his wife Ann.”

The Pegarania and the Traits

These two handwritten documents were compiled in 1848 and 1849 and represent a tremendous surge of energy, apparently driven by the need to put down on paper all he ever learned about life before it was too late. He was 74 years old and no doubt the death of his wife in 1847 was a factor. There is a line, early in the Pegarania, when he paraphrases the Book of Common Prayer: "Man that is born of woman hath but a short time to live, he is cut down like a flower and is no more seen".

The full title of the Pegarania is 'Pegarania or Thoughts on the Universe Together with the Popopulation (sic) of the Earth and the Religion of Mankind'. One suspects that even by 19th century standards the title was not exactly enticing. An accompanying letter to a publisher is dated 24 July 1849. The manuscript consists of 17 booklets, each made up of 5 sheets of paper, folded and neatly sewn in the middle so that each has a cover and 8 pages of text, which exactly fills all the area of the paper. His handwriting is consistent throughout and fully legible. In some of his other material, you realize that each subject takes up a page and comes to a conclusion exactly at the bottom right hand corner. After a while, it dawns on you that this apparently simple and mundane task has been achieved precisely every time– surely by a disciplined craftsman who acquired a skill of placing a subject within the confines of all sorts of shapes, spaces and curvatures.

The text itself is rather what you would expect from an auto-didactic. It starts with a List of Planets, continues with Geology, Vegetation, of Chaos, Moses and Creation, then an extensive catalogue of human behaviour (or rather misbehaviour), described and commented upon – Pride, Avarice, Persecution, Drunkenness, Idol Worship and so on and so on. Each later page has a heading – remember there are 136 pages in all – such as 'The Happiness of Man', 'The Inconsistencies of Religion', 'The Sabbath Day', 'Free Agency', 'The Worship of the Sun and Pandora's Box'. There is a note of all the popes from 606 to 1849. It finishes with 'The New Man'.

The Traits[*1] must also have been written in 1848 or 1849. This work does contain a digest of most of the autobiographical material from the Journal but it only occurs in snatches between poetry and religious commentary which could well have been included in the Pegarania. This time all the autobiographical content is in the third person – perhaps because subconsciously he has come to regard his life as finished and now a kind of dramatic fiction. The Library has a 19th century handwritten copy of the Traits by a Mr Robinson which (understandably) turns out to be a highly edited version.

Apart from these two main items, there is an assortment of other papers possibly delivered at Meetings, a few letters and poems with some earlier versions of the Pegarania material. One letter is of interest.

"Dear Mary Launder, Thou hast many things to learn, but thou art young and if thou manage thy time properly thou might do right in that particular. The Almighty's requirings are according to the abilities which we have received: those that have only one Tallent will only have that to improve; but he that has ten will be required to improve them all. But how shall we know and how much? Our giddiness must be turned to steadiness. We must have our seasons of retirement appointed wherein the Light of the Holy Ghost will show us what wants doing and what undoing".

This seems to me to describe exactly how Pegg answered this crucial question. He was pained but not persuaded by the assessments of others, and so spent hours in silent meditation, waiting for an indication or rather a feeling which came from outside himself, a divine inspiration. He was not searching for some kind of logical argument or justification. I am sure that this would be the end of the matter as far as he was concerned although he elaborated at length in the Traits. However, the temptation is too great to speculate on what factors might have come into play, whether he recognised them or not, and that is the subject of the next chapter.

Footnote

1. The title 'Traits' to describe the contents of his book would seem more natural in the nineteenth century than to modern readers. Nonetheless, the latest edition of The Shorter Oxford Dictionary gives this as its first definition: "A stroke of the pen or pencil: a short line: a touch in a picture. A line, passage or piece of writing." Emerson, writing at the same time as Pegg, called his book 'English Traits'. This suggests that the word, which might occur more readily to the artist Pegg, was, however, in fashion.

5: "Obeying The Glorious Call" and "The Fiery Trial"

The last chapter was given over to Pegg's own words. This section is an attempt to examine them, to assess his character, especially if it helps to explain the distinct character of his paintings and why, within the constraints of commercial demand and very limited subject matter, he should choose to depict his flowers in the way he did.

Bearing in mind his interpretation of the Parable of the Talents, we might ask what did Pegg regard as his talent? Perhaps we should not automatically assume that it was his ability as an artist. If we go on the basis of how much time and energy he devoted to his literary and theological exercises in the second half of his life – all by choice and not through economic necessity – there can only be one answer. We might assume that he stopped applying his skills to painting solely for religious qualms of conscience or because of failing eyesight, because he said so. An alternative explanation might be that he came to believe that china painting was not only a sinful act but a rather trivial one as well, a diversion no more worthy than shop-keeping, even if he chose to dramatize the rejection much later. I think we can easily dismiss the eyesight problem: anyone looking at the lengthy manuscripts he wrote up to the last year of his life, must realize that it was no hindrance at all. In any case, there are plenty of examples of artists who continued to work despite severe visual ailments or the surprising number of composers with hearing problems. If the creative urge is there, it overcomes practically everything short of total paralysis.

The qualms of conscience, of course, are another matter. However, in all the letters he wrote between 1806 and 1810 which have survived, I can find few references to his painting. The fact that he is obviously a good ceramic painter (how good is a question we will reserve for the last chapter) and knew he was and enjoyed it, might lead us to the conclusion that although he might claim that his religion made him abandon painting, actually lurking behind was some sort of painful satisfaction that self denial gave him. Following this rather speculative line, a thoroughly valid explanation would be that it was such a delicate and emotional subject for him that he blocked off any mention whatsoever, but, since he freely referred to many other temptations, that would suggest an extremely repressed and disturbed personality. And that, indeed, could be an accurate description.

It has already been suggested that the heights of elation and depths of despair which he described in his letters, in his Journal and in the final reckoning of the Traits, sound very like someone suffering from a bi-polar disorder. But they might also be regarded as perfectly reasonable responses to circumstances. Still, the question of his sanity bears examination. One 19th century writer had little doubt on this score: "He was a very erratic and changeable character and a religious enthusiast: indeed, judging from his writings, there can be little doubt that he was not, in all things, perfectly sane". For a start, it is clear that he was certainly not 'a very erratic and changeable character'. As Pegg repeats from time to time, he became a Quaker in 1800 and remained a committed Quaker for the rest of his life. His personality was consistent and, if there was a distinct contrast between the calm and the control of his external behaviour and the questioning fervour inside his head, it remained so throughout his life. After 1820 his life could hardly have been more steady and settled: we have no way of knowing exactly how much this was to do with the contribution of his wife but that must have been essential.

As for being 'a religious enthusiast' which our 19th century author clearly thought must indicate some degree of mental instability, indeed, he certainly was. If one is prepared to argue that to choose a religion as a practical method of sorting out and structuring one's entire life is a sign of mental instability then a large proportion of mankind is at least a little mad. Anyone taking this line needs to consider what is meant by 'mad'. The test is to draw a line between devoted religious belief and a religious obsession which drags you away from reality and affects your behaviour towards others in a harmful way. I would argue that Pegg passed this test. In one of the letters to his wife Pegg wrote: "I see that we can profess to love God and at the same time in reality love the world". Much of this has to do with his Quaker beliefs. Perhaps this helps to explain the attraction they had for him, the way he held on tight to them and was drawn to the more demanding interpretations of these beliefs. It seems to me that the Quaker message was that whatever spiritual revelations and knowledge you experience, these must not detach you from very specific rules of conduct. On the contrary, they must reinforce the morality of your social behaviour.

However, it is fair to assume that in his own time and amongst his fellow workers at least, he was regarded as very religious and a bit eccentric. In that environment the behaviour of his brother did not help him much. Thomas Pegg was a gilder at the factory. All John Haslem has to write about him concerns one event and, as far as I can see, reading between the lines, suggests a method Haslem must have used frequently to collect some of his information.

Picture a table covered with bottles and tankards, surrounded by a group of retired workmen. "Remember old Thomas Pegg? He told us he was going to gather all the Jews together and make a pilgrimage to Jerusalem. And where did he finish up? (The group in unison) "The Forester's Arms at Borrowash!" Shouts of "Good old Josuah the Prophet" and "Who's ready for another pint?"

If we agree that William Pegg might not have led the standard life of a craftsman painter but was acceptably sane and chose to run his life on precepts suggested by Quakers, we might go on to point out the aspects which he found particularly congenial because they blended in with his natural inclinations.

We have already noted how Haslem portrayed Pegg as a quiet, introverted, modest man. There is, of course, a strong element in Quaker beliefs of the value of silence, 'retirement', which surely attracted him. Fox had a particular hatred of idolatry and its power to contaminate. Later in this chapter, we will see in some detail how this extended to cover practically every form of artistic endeavour. Pursuing the same line of thought, Pegg regarded pride as a sort of self-idolatry. He persistently refers to the evil influence of pride. For example, in a letter of 1806, he wrote:"…it is hard to learn how to abound without being lifted up (I mean proud) as it is to learn how it is to want without being in despair". In the Journal he tells us that in 1799 "I burnt all my drawings, books and all (except a few drawings of flowers) even

Watts Hymns and Psalms, as I considered them the engines of will-worship." Practically at the beginning of the Pegarania, after a page headed ' All men are deficient in their mortal qualifications', we have pages headed 'Pride is a leading feature in the character of man', 'Pride and ignorance go hand in hand', and ' Pride is the forerunner of a multitude of evil'. I think he sees problems for anyone who achieves some degree of success in their chosen field, be it a creative art or the accumulation of wealth or social standing. This is indeed the very modern problem of celebrity – popular newspapers sell well when they point out fragilities in any public figure, no matter what the field of achievement happens to be. Pegg may have persuaded himself to take an extreme course to avoid the temptation of pride and was helped by the kind of atmosphere created in some Quaker communities.

There does seem to be an element in Quakerism which shuns publicity, something which may well cause a degree of conflict for the creative artist who usually wants to communicate as widely as possible. In recent times, this dilemma was considered by Donald Swann (of Flanders and Swann fame) who eventually became a Quaker. He found that when he spoke to Quakers about his concept of 'creative anonymity' "they understood it at once".

It is, however, worth remarking that there is a paradox, if not a clear contradiction, with Pegg. He may have been instinctively modest and very aware of the consequences of pride, but I am able to write pages and pages about him because he wrote pages and pages about himself and his ideas which he set out carefully and preserved – for posterity.

From time to time I have made the point that Pegg's Quakerism was of the more severe kind. I mean not just by our 21st century standards but also by his contemporary ones. To put it into context, we must recognize the preceding 150 years of Quaker customs and attitudes to the arts in general. It would be helpful to know what they were.[*1]

As always, Fox established the basic premises: his argument was that at worst most creative art leads to idolatry and at best it is a distraction in that it "burthens the pure life". Interestingly, he seems to have been totally unaware that he made an exception for one important art form, literature. His Journal, on the whole, is readable because of his flair for vigorous and frequently vivid metaphor. Pegg preserved an extract from Fox's Doctrinals in his papers presumably because it clearly sets out the principles he intended to follow. Most of it is in fact a direct quotation from the Book of Deuteronomy.

"Thou shall not make any graven image, or the similitude of any figure, the likeness of any male or female, or the likeness of any beast of the earth, or the likeness of any winged fowl in the air, or the likeness of any creeping thing on the ground, or the likeness of any fish in the waters."

In case the passage was misconstrued, Fox elaborates: "And thus you may see that they were forbidden making the likeness of anything in heaven and earth lest at the least they should come to worship the host of heaven. And thus you may see they were not only forbidden the worshipping of such things, but the making of likenesses of them, by the express command of God".

It could be argued that in the ur-text in Deuteronomy there is no mention of the depiction of plants (perhaps an oversight by God).

William Penn and Robert Barclay specifically endorsed Fox's prohibitions.

Eighteenth century and nineteenth century Quakers had a particular aversion to portraiture – and considerable soul searching when photography arrived. There was also a similar aversion to colour, even though Fox and the early titans did not specifically condemn it. Their clothes seem to have been uniformly grey, brown or, very occasionally, green. Clarkson, who wrote 'Portraiture of Quakerism' in 1806, summed it up: "All gay colours, such as red, blue, green and yellow are exploded". Bearing in mind that strict Quaker tradition selected these two aspects of visual art for special condemnation, it is interesting that the sketch book (now preserved in the Crown Derby Museum) which Pegg prepared immediately after his return to Derby in 1813, has some very bright colours. A small portrait came to light at the same time as the sketch book and is now in a private collection. It conforms to the description he gives of himself at the time, long hair and a beard, so seems very likely to be a self-portrait. He also dares to include paintings of insects.

Despite all the very substantial support which Quaker founding fathers and probably the majority of 18th and 19th century households would have given the position Pegg adopted, it must be stressed that he could have found other equally committed Quakers who, quite comfortably, would have allowed him to continue with his profession. Even Margaret Fell – Mrs. Fox – wrote: "Christ Jesus saith that we must take no thought what we shall eat, or what we shall drink, or what we shall put on: but bids us consider the lilies, how they grow in more royalty than Solomon. But contrary to this, we must look at no colours, nor make anything that is changeable colours as the hills are, nor sell them nor wear them: but we must be all in one dress and one colour. This is a silly poor gospel."

By 1798 William Savery, an American visitor to England, remarked that there were two types of Quakers here, 'plain Friends' and 'gay Friends'. Elizabeth Fry and her family, the Gurneys, accentuated the disparity in the first half of the 19th century, when 'Gurneyism', a more liberal interpretation of the faith, became the hot discussion topic of the day in Britain and America.[*2]

There seems to have been no strong antipathy towards drawing; it was even encouraged and was introduced into the curriculum of Quaker schools in the early 19th century, long before it was adopted by other educational establishments. As far as the profession of artist is concerned, the court painter and President of the Royal Academy throughout the whole time Pegg was agonising about whether to follow his craft or not, was Benjamin West. He came from a Quaker family in Pennsylvania and, while not a practising Quaker, never repudiated his Quakerism and was regarded as a Quaker by George III and the high class intellectual elite he mixed with.

Examining the local scene, we note that Thomas Martin Randall was a well known shell painter and, as a Quaker friend of Pegg, was the recipient of the 1813 Sketchbook. The Howitts were the stalwarts of the Heanor Meeting and considerable literary figures in their day.[*3] Late in life, Mary Howitt described her resentment as a child when her father burned a particularly fine flower painting since it was "better not to indulge in colours". Mary even provides evidence that Pegg was not under excessive pressure from his local Quaker community. After she and her husband William moved to Kingston in Surrey in 1836, she noted:" The Kingston Friends seemed narrow and severe…It was so different from the pleasant, tolerant ways of the Nottingham Quakers". (Her dissatisfaction lingered apparently since she ended her life as a Roman Catholic).

To return to the effect of Quaker beliefs on William Pegg, it seems important to point out that the Society was formed as a direct rejection of many aspects of other religious practices. While George Fox was prepared to condemn the whole structure and rituals of the established churches and this included the Church of England, the assertions of faith, philosophy and practices at the other extreme end of the spectrum belonged to the Roman Catholic Church. The distinctly different approaches to the matter of personal misconduct is a case in point. Both creeds adopted the course of guilt established by proof (usually admission), censure and withdrawal of full membership with the promise of redemption. However, the Quakers enforced this much more rigorously by group decision and not within the confidentiality of the confessional, administered by a single individual (the priest). In visual terms, the differences between the places of worship could hardly be more extreme. Compare the Derby Meetinghouse, typically austere inside and outside, with the Rococo churches in France and Germany. The fact was that Derby Porcelain drew inspiration from the Sevres and Meissen factories. While Pegg never visited the Continent (indeed, for most of the time from his arrival in Derby in 1795 to his final years at the Derby factory, Britain was at war with France – a fact never mentioned in his letters) he would probably have regarded the Continent as essentially Roman Catholic territory. This is speculation, because Pegg never explicitly said so, but I wonder if this is a partial explanation of why he felt such an emotionally charged reaction to the specific objects that he helped to produce. Perhaps, on first arriving from Stoke, he gave little thought to what he was moving into, but for five years he was immersed nearly every day in the factory, surrounded by objects which are not only frivolous (think of the number of figures without even the semblance of practical use) but extreme and constant reminders of the sort of culture he specifically rejected (we may not necessarily think of culture in religious terms but he certainly did). After a similar length of time at his second spell of employment, the misgivings returned.

There is the element that I think Pegg might recognise in one form but I am fairly certain would not accept the speculation that flows from it. Indeed, he would have been appalled. Look at his paintings, the way they fill the surface to be decorated, they flourish, even sometimes breaking into the gilding round the rim and that applies to the watercolours as well. I fail to see how you can avoid the conclusion that the exuberance and the drama could only be achieved by someone who is enjoying considerable emotional satisfaction from what he is doing. For want of a better word, they are exciting. My suspicion is that such pleasure subsequently disturbs him, he even feels ashamed. Here is where the danger of pseudo-psychology may take over but I draw a little confidence from the fact that John Twitchett (someone who has devoted more attention to Pegg than anyone since Haslem) has been drawn down the same track and uses the word 'erotic'.

Consider Pegg's life. We have a shy, sensitive child brought up in firmly religious home, welcoming biblical texts with their strongly advocated sexual codes. He arrives in Derby, eventually chooses a potential wife but has to reject her and apparently doesn't look for a substitute while he undergoes years of immense physical and mental hardship. ('Fornication' and 'Marrying Outside the Society' are the two most cited 'offences' in the Quaker archive.) Back in Derby, practically the first thing he does is to find himself a wife. He launches himself into his craft, defiantly ignoring Quaker reservations about it. I am unaware of Ann Headley's age but there were certainly no children of the marriage. He is a devoted husband but do the letters written to his wife four years later reveal tensions not wholly related to painting? I think we should stop there – except to quote from one of his letters: "The strongholds of sin, the lust of the flesh, the lust of the eye." The latter was his favoured term for painting which he probably adapted from the New Testament by way of St. Augustine of Hippo.

I should also reveal that I did not give all of the quotation from the Journal where he described his unkempt appearance on his return to Derby. This is the full version: "During this time I wore my beard. I was not shaved within the year from the time I neglected to do it: but it was not altogether neglect, it was intended as a testimony against effeminacy". Make what you will of that.

Before these speculations about the poor man's sexuality, mainly on the basis of the way he paints flowers, get out of hand, a note of caution is necessary, provided by another flower painter. The American artist Georgia O'Keeffe made a series of surprisingly similar flower studies in the 1920s and 30s which drew comments from critics about the sexual connotations they recognised in them. "You hung all your own associations with flowers on my flower, and you write about my flower as if I think and see what you think and see of the flower – and I don't", she said. She furiously refused to discuss the subject in interviews.

For a final conclusion about whatever it was that drove Pegg in and out of his brief painting career, it is worth considering the Traits, probably written two years or so before his death.

It is not easy to 'understandeth what thou readest', with its jumble of scriptural comment, Old Testament genealogies, Pegg family history (in Norman times!), personal history, poetry and more besides. The best approach is to regard it as a kind of poor man's 'Apologia Pro Vita Sua' – except that Newman wrote his book sixteen years later. His opening description of himself as 'that Persecuted Man' is at first a bit puzzling if you assume it was because he was a Quaker. By this time the Society had come to a reasonable accommodation with the rest of the comunity. However, after many pages, near the end, his meaning emerges. "When the light was clear and his convictions strong and was sure beyond all doubt that God was requiring his sacrifice at his hands, then he warned of the consequence that would follow rebellion, that his candlestick would be removed out of its place and condemnation of Saul would follow: under these feelings death seemed more desirable than life". Pegg then takes up a page about the general concept of persecution, followed by "When a man becomes a persecutor he exposes his own weakness but when he resigns himself into the hands of God, then the wicked will persecute him also."

It seems that the Traits was conceived as an answer to all those who criticised him for the life choices he had made, in particular for giving up painting. He wrote in his Journal: "In thus giving way to the feelings of conscience I experienced great opposition: my friends, as far as I could see, all turned against me, so that I had a heavy burden to bear". However, as we have noted, there were plenty of Quakers who would have supported him for each choice he made but not necessarily the same people, although, amongst his Derby Friends, those of the more permissive persuasion appear to have been in the majority. In any case, if they disapproved of the transformation from top class painter into small-time shopkeeper, they were prepared to help him out when the project was sliding into debt. It appears, in fact, that the chief persecutor was Pegg himself. At the conclusion of the Traits he writes: "The Friend of whom these traits portray the feelings of his mind, was not guided by these scriptural phrases but by the feelings of his own mind purely".

In the end, it would appear that he dramatised the account of his life: "the subject of these Traits is written in the third person which mode seems most proper to the writer of them". In the same way, he dramatised his flowers. Give him a plate and give him a flower, leave him to his own devices, and he would produce a dramatic and flamboyant statement.

Footnotes

1. Most of the following material comes from 'Quakers And The Arts' by Frederick J. Nicholson (1968) which is a comprehensive survey of the changing approach within the Society of Friends to all the creative arts right up to the mid 20th century.

2. In 1869 a group of Quakers at Fritchley, a village in the hills10 miles north of Derby, established a Meeting, semi-detached from the Annual London Meeting, essentially on a 'back to basics' agenda and only became fully attached again in 1962. I guess that Pegg would have become a loyal member: a tract in his papers, probably dating from his last years, enquires "Had George Fox been told that his disciples could re-establish the day of the Sun and the War Principle and Free Agency, what would he have said?"

3. Amongst Mary Howitt's contributions to English literature is:
"Will you walk into my Parlour?" Said a spider to a fly
"T'is the prettiest little parlour that ever you did spy".

6: Pegg's Gifts

This study of Quaker Pegg could be said to have four elements. We might have a special interest in Quaker ideas and history. We might be inspired by considering local history – there is something rather magical about standing in a field beside an isolated farmhouse or looking at a weed-covered patch at the back of a cowshed and imagining the scene 350 years before when dozens, perhaps even hundreds of people, would make their way across the fields to converge on these tiny pieces of land. We could look across at the Guildhall in Derby Market Square and think that in that space an irate local worthy first spat out the word 'Quaker' which became part of our language ever afterwards. We might even be quite interested in the profuse and sprawling writings of a tortured "religious enthusiast" who, during the first half of the 19th century, gave up his job because of his religious principles. All well and good, but what takes Pegg's story on to another plane is the fact that he produced work we can see and admire and, depending on your opinion, may well be, in a limited field, amongst the finest artistic achievements of his day. Of course, the key questions are; how good, how exceptional and how original was he?

Before we attempt an answer, I think it is important to give some idea of the sheer technical ability required before he, and all the other ceramic artists, could paint anything on the glaze for us to judge. A layman might think that decorating china for Pegg was much the same process as a painter uses on canvas or a water-colourist on paper. To give an idea of the kind of skill, experience and knowledge required in a very special technique, we can do no better than quote from an account by Arnold Machin of the procedures he watched, working in the Minton Factory in the 1930s. Arnold Machin, it should be said, followed a career not unlike John Haslem's. He learned his craft of ceramic painting and modelling with Mintons and later at Royal Crown Derby before he moved to London where he developed his sculpture and then returned to teach in Derby. If the success of a portrait- maker is judged by the number of times the work is reproduced, Machin is the most successful portrait-maker in the history of the world. He designed the Queen's head on our stamps and coinage.

'To apply gold or colour to highly glazed ware required very precise skill and knowledge of how to adjust the colour. I was most intrigued by the arrangement which enabled the gilders to make these fine adjustments. Each operative was supplied with a cup and saucer; the required colour was put into the saucer and turpentine poured into the cup and allowed to overflow; because the turpentine was more thinly spread in the saucer, evaporation increased and gradually the colour began to thicken. This was known as 'fat oil'. At the end of each day the cup was topped up and again allowed to overflow, replacing the turpentine which had evaporated during the day. Eventually another saucer was placed under the first, separated from it by three bits of wood about half-an-inch thick, then another, and another, until each saucer contained fat oil of different grades of viscosity. Some of the older workers had as many as six saucers, enabling them to produce colours and textures of amazing variety.

A touch of glycerine was sometimes added when working on long strokes and aniseed oil was also used in order to keep the colour 'open' and facilitate application; in fact, aniseed was the dominant smell in the painting and gilding shops. Another type of oil was used to dry up the colour. The colours came in powdered form but although they were already finely ground, each operative ground them again on a tile with the turpentine. He would start the day by mixing the colours he required with a palette knife at the top of the tile ready for use, covering them with a saucer to keep them soft and to prevent dust from settling.'

I would doubt whether these processes had changed much within the previous century and Pegg would surely have recognised most if not all of them.

Reminding you again, do not assume that the technique is the same as applying paint to canvass, when the artist stands back eventually to see a final result which has been entirely under his control. The ceramic artist does not have such satisfaction at that point. He would have had to anticipate what the firing process would do to those smears of paint which, at that moment, only bore some resemblance to the finished work and might require up to four separate firings to fix or correct certain colours.

Finally, a word about the kiln operators. My friend, John Fineran, has kindly provided the following description of the process that would have been followed at the time. "With no electronic temperature gauges, they had to assess the state of a glaze firing lasting 12 hours or longer. Traditionally firing of china was primarily judged by looking at the colour of the heat in the 'hovel' (we would say, kiln). The hovel was surrounded by the much larger structure, the bottle oven. Cherry red inclining to orange would indicate the higher temperature values and would be visible through spy holes in the thick refractory brickwork of the kiln. Small samples of glazed body would also be drawn from the holes to note the development of the body, glaze or colours. A greater quantity of coal was used in the early stages but reduced as the atmosphere cleared and steam and carbonaceous matter was burnt off. Upon reaching the required temperature the fires would be starved of fuel, all openings clammed up and the kiln allowed to cool slowly to avoid fracture of the ware, glaze spoliation or even collapse."

Such a series of judgements by experienced eyes over many hours produced the kind of surface and glaze most of us probably take for granted.

When one looks at the photographs in the literature, it becomes clear that, while some items are positively identified as Pegg's work, others are 'possibly by' or ' attributed to' him. It is clear that there is an element in the house style at Derby Porcelain, which dates back at least to Billingsley, that Pegg seems to have exploited but might just as well have been taken up by other painters as required. It is always well to remember that he was not a free agent but a commercial artist whose output was determined to a greater or lesser extent by the demands of the market. All this can be graphically demonstrated by the Pineapple Dishes displayed in the Charles Norman Collection at the Usher Art Gallery in Lincoln.

Without having to visit Lincoln (though well worth the effort), it is possible to follow the development of the design and decoration in available publications. In 'Painters and the Derby China Works' page 49 is a design by Billingsley for a centre comport or fruit dish. Plate XXI on page 117 shows it apparently realised for a piece in the Castle Howard Collection. Consult the Second Supplementary Catalogue for the Charles Norman Collection and you will see two Pineapple Dishes with shapes and decorations almost identical with the original Billingsley design. One dish is painted by

Billingsley and the other by Pegg. These two dishes vary only slightly: the treatment of the leaves by Pegg is more detailed and he has added a spray of forget-me-nots on each side of the drain hole in the concave. A suggested date for the Billingsley dish is 1795 and 1796 for Pegg's. Billingsley left the Factory in April 1796 and Pegg joined in the autumn of that year. A plausible explanation is that Pegg was detailed to produce a version of the already existing Billingsley dish in order to make a pair. On this evidence at least, it is not unreasonable to think that the style was not Pegg's innovation and although he might have exploited it, he was not alone. The paintings on china by Joseph Bancroft, in particular ('Painters and the Derby China Works' pages 96 – 116) illustrate the point – though in his case he arrived at the Factory after Pegg and was probably directly influenced by him. Perhaps questionable attributions could be marked 'School of Pegg'. This is not an entirely fanciful suggestion because there actually was a School of Pegg. This paragraph is a late addition at the end of Haslem's book, the result of an interview in 1875 with James Rowse who worked in the same room as Pegg.

"William Pegg he describes as always having been kind to the apprentices to flower painting, and taking pleasure in giving them instructions in his art. At night, when the day's work at the factory was over, Rowse and others of the boys, were in the habit of attending at Pegg's house, where he seemed to take great pleasure in giving them lessons, the only recompense he would receive for his trouble, being the drawings they did under his tuition."

While it is assumed, because of Pegg's careful sketch book studies and indeed the Thistle Plate, that he preferred to work directly from nature, (as indeed did Billingsley) it is also a fact that, like many of his fellow artists, he could refer to books of botanical illustrations – for example, Curtis's Botanical Journal and 'The Artist's Repository' which he had in his possession when an apprentice.

It becomes obvious that it is misguided to let Pegg take credit for all the best florid painting (is there a better or more appropriate word than florid?). Haslem (who obviously knew a bit about marketing) anticipated this problem, especially when details of Pegg's unusual life became known: "more flowers will be attributed to his brush than he could possibly have done, had he passed the whole of his life at the painting bench". Consequently, the next question is, how have positive identifications been established?

The very basic evidence is provided by marks to be found on the underside or base of the porcelain. These at least establish that we are looking at a piece of Derby China and something produced during the periods when Pegg was employed at the factory. Charts showing the marks are given in Haslem and Twitchett's books. Through our relevant period they usually consisted of a crown above a St. Andrews cross with three dots each side of it and, underneath, a D (in copperplate style). Around 1806 and subsequently, these marks are normally red but previously they could be rose, blue or puce coloured. The gilders, who were responsible not only for the decorations in gold, as the name implies, but usually for the pattern, if any, around the rim, had marks (usually numbers) incised into the clay. Haslem, followed by Twitchett, warned against reading too much into marks since they were simply there to identify, if necessary, the particular workmen responsible; the codes could be changed at any time and only accurately interpreted by contemporary employees.

The painters, on the whole, were not identified on the pieces. Haslem again: "It was not the practice of the painters in Billingsley's day to put their names on their work". It was, however, common practice to write details of the subjects, whether they were flowers, plants or landscapes, with the mark. It is possible to recognize Pegg's handwriting on pieces (although modern eyes may not find it too easy to discriminate between examples of 19th century handwriting). Derby Porcelain has another extensive documentary source, the Pattern Books, itemised designs compiled for about thirty years up to 1810, which are now deposited at Derby Museum and Art Gallery (details are printed in Twitchett 'Derby Porcelain' (2002)). Painters are sometimes specified but Pegg is only mentioned three times ('Flowers by Peg'(sic) in the Tea Book I 475 and in the Plate Book 239 and 240). Of course, the Pattern Books only cover his first period of employment.

Disregarding all this, I convince myself that I can tell a piece by Pegg when I see it which, of course, is a very dubious means of authoritative identification. Haslem does give a crumb of comfort: 'China painters know each others work as well as people in general know the handwriting of their friends and acquaintances' – 'With the painters of landscapes, flowers, fruit or birds, this recognition is still easier, as one painter has a liking for certain flowers, another for a particular style of subject, and they have each a manner of their own in treating them'.

However, there is one piece that is authentically Pegg's in every sense. We are back to where we started with the Thistle Dish. He chose the subject, he chose the colours, he showed the painting to Thomas Soar and, while he may not have selected the base plate, he settled for little or no elaboration for the rim. I realise that, on first sight, while my interest might, later on, have been increased by the information on the accompanying label, this piece itself made an immediate impact. I think I saw something special in his work, and I still do.

How good is he? Opinions vary from 'a tolerably clever painter' to (normally) 'one of the best Derby China painters'. As a layman, I am consoled, however, by reading the assessment of John Twitchett who must have seen more painted china-ware than most and more Quaker Pegg pieces than most. He has written: "William Pegg the Quaker was, in the opinion of the writer, the finest flower painter to have learnt or practised his art at the Derby China Manufactory, and indeed in the ceramic industry as a whole."

If you agree that Pegg's decorations have 'something special', with their drama, clarity and intensity, perhaps this lengthy attempt may help to explain how and why this came about. I think it is clear that his work becomes more wild and emotional under the impact of the Quaker experience, which must date from the exact time the Thistle Dish was painted, and this became the distinctive characteristic of his second period. When he painted, his Quaker convictions told him 'You should not be doing this, but since you are, you must do it with honesty and integrity to the very best of your ability'. What we see is the outcome of a painful struggle to deny his instincts and to suppress a vision because the process of trying to communicate it would become a wholly self-satisfying substitute for true worship. The power of that vision was described by his contemporary, an artist who also had 'such an inclination for writing', but with none of Pegg's inhibitions, William Blake:

'To see a World in a Grain of Sand
And a Heaven in a Wild Flower'.

.....and perhaps also, the Flames of Hell.

Suggestions for Further Study

It is possible to see Pegg's work at the Derby Art Gallery where several of his pieces are on permanent display (the gallery has 28 in its entire collection). The Royal Crown Derby Museum has on display a duplicate of the Thistle Plate which Pegg made in 1813, and another plate, together with the sketchbook. The Usher Gallery at Lincoln has 10 examples, part of the Charles Norman Collection, on exhibition. The Collection is confined to pieces from about 1775 to 1805 so does not have work from Pegg's second period. A fine catalogue by Anthony Hope has been published where every piece is illustrated in colour and described in detail. The Trustees of the collection publish supplementary catalogues from time to time and at present three are available. The Ashmolean Museum in Oxford has a version of the Thistle Plate on display. There are probably other examples in public collections.

Many pieces are in private collections. (A useful list of Derby Porcelain collectors in general is given in Twitchett (2002) p.14-16). A dessert service was exhibited at the premises of Albert Amor in London in1979 and over 40 pieces were sold as separate items, so is presumably well dispersed. An article in the London Illustrated News dated November 19 1979 provides details and some photographs.

Apart from the Charles Norman Collection Catalogue, there are plentiful illustrations in publications but by far the best and the most extensive appear in the two editions of 'Derby Porcelain' by John Twitchett. The first edition (1980) has a full text together with a list of items in the 1813 Sketchbook. The second edition of 'Derby Porcelain' (2002) has less text on Pegg and different illustrations. An article by him on the discovery of the Sketch books appeared in the Antique Collector Vol 6 1983. He is co-author with John Murdoch of 'Painters and the Derby China Works' (1987), also recommended.

F. Brayshaw Gilhesby in his ‘Derby Porcelain’ (p. 87) has a quaint anecdote about finding a Pegg lid in bombed-out Plymouth.

And, of course, we have John Haslem’s ‘The Old Derby China Factory’.

The Derby Porcelain International Society issues regular publications on Derby Porcelain and other Derbyshire ceramics of all periods, as well as organising a wide variety of events. The address of the Membership Secretary is Box No. 6997, Coleshill, Warwickshire, B46 2LF U.K.

Bibliography

Barrett, F.A. and Thorpe, A.L., Derby Porcelain (Faber and Faber 1971).

Forde, Helen. Derbyshire Quakers 1650-1761. Ph.D. Thesis Leicester University 1977.

Fox, George, The Journal of George Fox. Revised edition by John L. Nickalls (Cambridge 1952).

Gilhesby F. Brayshaw, Derby Porcelain (Macgibbon and Kee 1961).

Haslem, John, The Old Derby China Factory: The Workmen and Their Productions (1876). (Republished 1973, EP Publishing Ltd.)

Hoyte, Anthony, Catalogue of the Charles Norman Collection 1996 (with Supplementary Catalogues I (1999), II (2000), III (2006).

Machin, Arnold. Artist of an Icon. The Memoirs of Arnold Machin R.A. (Frontier Publishing 2002).

Murdoch, John and Twitchett, John, Painters and the Derby China Works, (Trefoil 1987).

Nicholson, Frederick J., Quakers and the Arts (Friends Home Service Committee 1968).

Twitchett, John, Derby Porcelain (Hutchinson 1980).

Twitchett, John, Derby Porcelain (Antique Collectors' Club 2002).

Appendix

The Quakers from the Mid 17th to Mid 19th Centuries

Although the history of the Society of Friends, the Quakers, must begin at the middle of the 17th century with George Fox, it would be wrong to regard him simply as 'the onlie begetter'. Fox was, in fact, a catalyst – an extremely successful one – who brought together a large number of individuals and small groups, widely dispersed throughout the country. For a century, from the time of the Reformation and even before, such authority as institutionalised religion had possessed, endured challenges and contradictions, not least because whatever ostensible religious practice was in favour was likely to fluctuate from one royal generation to the next. In addition, by the time Fox actively started on his mission, the authority of the monarchy was not only challenged but was in the process of being eliminated – albeit temporarily.

However, the history of the Quakers for most of the17th century is, for all intents and purposes, the story of George Fox. This is because in 1676 towards the end of his life, Fox wrote down an incredibly detailed account of his part in the development of the Society where he notes practically every place he visited, large and small, anything of note that happened there, together with the names of the local people he encountered. The ground covered by his Journal can be measured by the fact that he was in effect a full time itinerant preacher for nearly 40 years, working his way through all the counties of England many times, and eventually venturing not only into Wales, Scotland and Ireland but also Holland, Germany, the West Indies and America.

In the first few years of his mission, Fox spent most of his time within thirty miles or so of Derby and so local and national Quaker history amounts to one and the same thing. Because of its local interest, it is worth devoting the most space to those formative years between 1647 and 1652 but it must be said that this pattern of itinerant preaching, court hearings, painful, sometimes prolonged but always ineffectual imprisonment, divine retribution for his oppressors and ever increasing numbers of converts, is repeated throughout the rest of his Journal.

Fox was born and brought up in Drayton-in-the-Clay (today Fenny Drayton) in 1624. He presents himself as a sensitive and thoughtful child living in modest circumstances. His father was a weaver and Fox himself worked for a shoemaker and cattle-dealer until he was 19. The specific incident which finally convinced him to break away from the standard everyday life of an ordinary working-man, occurred when he found himself, in the course of his employment, joining a group at a fair. The procedure was that drinks were ordered on the basis that whoever was the first to refuse a refill, had to pay for everything consumed. When he realised this, he abruptly put down a contribution and left the scene. The scene served to symbolise everything he wanted to reject in this world and, in a short time, he distanced himself as far as he could from it. He abandoned his home, his relatives and his employment and began a travelling preaching career he sustained for more than 40 years.

At first he mainly moved around his home area in Leicestershire and Warwickshire but by 1647 this had extended to Derbyshire and Nottinghamshire. His very first named convert anywhere was Elizabeth Hooton of Skegby in Nottinghamshire. Before long he was up against the forces of law and order. These were turbulent times anyway when judges and magistrates must have wondered who was the next to be removed from office and possibly exterminated. No wonder that the local judiciary felt that they needed to act against someone who not only noisily challenged the local clergy and disrupted church services but also warned 'excise men to take heed of oppressing the poor' and was clearly gathering supporters around him. Fox names 'Eaton, a town near Derby' [*1] as the first place where converts gathered together in sufficient numbers to constitute a Meeting. 'And many were moved by the Lord to go to steeplehouses (his word for church buildings) to the priests and to the people, to declare the everlasting truth unto them'. In 1649 he was briefly in prison in Nottingham. Despite following his disruptive activities in Leicestershire and Warwickshire, he seems to have been relatively unscathed, but, back in Nottinghamshire and Derbyshire the next year, he was put in the stocks at Mansfield Woodhouse, thrown out of Chesterfield and finished up in October 1650 being arrested for blasphemy in Derby.

From that moment, he was, as he put it, 'kept a year within three weeks, in four prisons, the House of Corrections and the town prison and the county gaol and dungeon and then in the high gaol where I was kept till I was set free at liberty'. Brought before the court at Derby, he faced one of the presiding magistrates, Gervase Bennett of Snelston who had the distinction of being the first to give members of the Society of Friends the more colloquial title of Quakers. It was said that this was because Fox 'bid (the justices) to tremble at the word of God'. One suspects that Bennett might also have been influenced by Fox's physical performance in front of him. In a much later part of his Journal, Fox reports, apparently verbatim, the comment of a Lancashire judge: "I will not be afraid of thee, George Fox, thou speakest so loud, thy voice drowns mine and the Court's; I must call for three or four criers to drown thy voice, thou hast good lungs".

While in custody, Fox set about bombarding the local clergy, the magistrates, the mayor, the court and even the bell-ringers at St. Peter's church with letters, all reproduced in his Journal. Presumably he preserved copies for the rest of his life as part of an extensive archive – or perhaps they were simply returned unopened.

While one is not supposed to have much sympathy for Bennett, it is easy to see why he became excessively frustrated with such an intensely troublesome prisoner inside and outside the court and was anxious to be rid of him as quickly as possible. He obviously thought he had at last solved his problems when Fox's relatives and others in Derby were prepared to put forward over £150 (a massive sum) as a surety so that Fox could be bound- over and thereby released. Fox, of course, refused to acknowledge any guilt or any promise of future behaviour and proceeded to kneel down and pray that God would forgive Bennett for his sins. At this point, whatever self-control Bennett possessed, simply snapped. "He ran upon me with both his hands and struck me and cried, 'Away with him, gaoler. Take him away, gaoler'."

It so happened that in August 1651 Cromwell's army was passing through the Derby area on their way to what became the Battle of Worcester. A desperate search for any able-bodied recruits automatically included prisons and Fox, with clear leadership qualities, was offered a commission which he naturally refused. This apparently prompted the frustrated Bennett to send constables to Fox offering him freedom and money if he was willing to join the army as a private soldier. This particular incident came in useful many years later when, after the Restoration of Charles II, Fox was in court for refusing to take an Oath of Allegiance to the king. He was able to say that, while he objected to swearing any oaths, he was a fully loyal subject of Charles II and 'Judge Bennett cast me into a dungeon because I would not take up arms against the King (father of Charles II) and be a captain.'

As Fox points out, the judiciary 'could not agree what to do with me'. He had been charged with a changing variety of offences, had been moved from one place to another and had become an exasperating embarrassment. "At length they were made to turn me out of gaol about the beginning of winter in the year 1651". His parting letter to the Derby Magistrates ends: ' It doth break my heart to see how God is dishonoured in thee, o Derby'.

Shortly before his release he had written: 'I saw that when the Lord should bring me forth, it would be as the letting of a lion out of a den amongst the wild beasts of the forest'. One could hardly improve on that as a description of his subsequent career. We have already noted the incredible vitality of the man as he travelled more or less perpetually for the next 30 years, encouraging the faithful, defying the law, suffering imprisonment, spreading his gospel. He returned to Derbyshire and the surrounding counties regularly but no more regularly than to anywhere else in England. His performance was rather like the classic Chinese circus artist who keeps a large number of saucers spinning on sticks by dashing from one to the next to give it a twirl.

In the next few years, while Fox's activities were always dispersed, they began to be focused or rather centralised on Cumbria. The reason was that in 1652 he was given a surprisingly warm welcome in the home of Judge Fell and his wife Margaret. Although a family of considerable local status, they were by no means immune from persecution but they and their children remained wholly loyal to Fox and his mission for the rest of his life. The Judge died in 1658 and Fox married his widow in 1669.

In the meantime, the Restoration of the Monarchy in 1660 marked a distinct increase in the prosecution of non-conformists and in 1662 an Act was passed specifically against Quakers. There followed a series of laws, collectively known as the Clarendon Code, which attempted to encourage attendance at the established Church of England and severely restrict the activities of those with other religious persuasions. Thousands of Quakers were imprisoned. However, within a year of James II's accession in 1685, pardons were issued and prisoners released from gaol (apparently through very active lobbying by Fox and friends). Soon after William and Mary were installed, the Toleration Act of 1689 removed many of the legal restraints suffered by Quakers.

Significantly, the years of oppression up to the early 1680s marked the maximum British membership of the Society, possibly for all time in actual numbers, and definitely as a percentage of the population, (perhaps providing a salutary lesson for politicians, past and present). It was estimated that by 1680 there were 80,000 Quakers and in some areas they represented a considerable part of the population – for example, an estimated 10% in Bristol.

Three other major developments took place in Fox's lifetime (he died in 1691). The first was initiated by Fox himself and was elaborated in later years. He gave a cohesive structure by requiring regular fixed attendances with a Monthly Meeting in addition to weekly religious observance. Each group (confusingly called a Meeting) nominated representatives to a regional body, a Quarterly Meeting, and likewise this group nominated representatives to a national Annual Meeting. This structure, slightly modified, still exists, probably because it has generally been successful in creating a comprehensive method of communication and a sense of democratic collective responsibility.

The second significant step took place when William Penn acquired an estate in America that became Pennsylvania. The option of emigrating to the New World where dissenters imagined they could follow their favoured religious practices without interference from the state, had been available from the start of the century but this development on this scale with specific encouragement for Quakers, set a precedent. It became a factor in the declining number of Quakers in Britain for at least the following 200 years.

The third important event was the publication of Robert Barclay's 'An Apology for the True Christian Divinity' in 1678. This was a classic theological work that in a sense codified Quaker principles and doctrines, giving them an academic and theological respectability. It became something of a Quaker bible. His severe restatement of a rejection of 'frivolous recreations' applied not only to gambling and alcohol but also to almost all the arts.

The 18th century can be covered in a few lines. Membership of the Society slowly decreased. No one attempted to emulate Fox's aggressive and highly active missionary methods – his natural successor in this respect, was surely John Wesley. On the whole the Quakers seemed more inclined to look inwards, focussing on personal standards of belief and behaviour. Converts were attracted by example. This rather exclusive tendency (at least in the eyes of the outside world) was enhanced by their austere approach to outward appearances both for their dress and their Meeting Houses. However, if they appeared to withdraw from society in this respect, they increasingly engaged in practical terms by promoting education, the care of prisoners and care of the poor. They were excluded from the professions and Parliament but this had the effect of channelling their talents into trade and industry where their reputation for probity and their abstemious habits led some to substantial wealth which could be invested in these projects.

In the 19th century, slowly, but not without opposition from within the Society itself, a less isolated stance was adopted. In the twenty years after Pegg's death, the Annual Meetings decided that gravestones were permitted and Quakers were allowed to marry outside the Membership, while Parliament removed whatever legal restrictions remained and Quakers gained full citizenship. The national Membership reported in 1847 was15,345.

We can now turn to the local situation from the 18th century through Pegg's lifetime, to the mid 19th century. The history of the Quakers in Derbyshire from 1650 to 1761 (when the Derbyshire membership was amalgamated with Nottinghamshire) has been helpfully covered in comprehensive and meticulous detail by Helen Forde in her Ph. D thesis. She concludes that the membership was mostly confined to the less affluent, such as yeoman farmers and wholesalers, with few, if any, wealthy patrons. Even in the harshest years in the 17th century, despite Fox's experience, the general attitude of the authorities was moderate in the face of incitement from the clergy. Following the national trend, numbers declined in the 18th century. Forde calculates that in Derbyshire there were 216 Members between 1660-69: 573 between 1690-99: 160 by 1750.[*2] Quaker members were more numerous and particularly active in Monyash and Chesterfield. Derby itself was virtually dormant until it revived in the last decade of the century. There were two sustained Meetings in the south of the county, however, at Furnace near Oakerthorpe and Whiteley or White-lee, later to be named Breach, on the border of Denby and Codnor.

Forde makes the interesting observation that they were possibly located in these two places, rather than in the more agricultural areas, because these were mining communities. Certainly the landscape during the 18th and 19th centuries must have been pock-marked with shallow mineral extraction, since coal seams were discovered relatively near the surface (as were iron ore and ceramic clay deposits) which individuals and small groups could exploit before deep-shaft collieries were developed.[*3]

Footnotes

1. Ernest Watkins identifies this as the modern Little Eaton.

2. Figures can be confusing. These are for those who were adopted as committed Members of the Meetings. There were also birthright Quakers, the children of parents who were both Members. Gatherings for religious observance at Meeting Houses could include many who attended but were not Members.

3. Commenting in 1909, Watkins wrote: "The whole country from Heanor to Belper is terribly disfigured and the atmosphere poisoned, probably both quite needlessly, but by present methods of coal-getting and iron-smelting. Coming through this now horrible but once beautiful region where it is a consolation to think that these disfigurements and abominations must some day pass away." Thankfully, that day has arrived.